CONTEMPORARY ART

FROM CRESCENT MOON PUBLISHING

The Art of Andy Goldsworthy
by William Malpas

The Art of Andy Goldsworthy
by William Malpas

Andy Goldsworthy: Touching Nature
by William Malpas

Andy Goldsworthy In Close-Up
by William Malpas

The Art of Richard Long
by William Malpas

Constantin Brancusi: Sculpting the Essence of Things
by James Pearson

Alison Wilding: The Embrace of Sculpture
by Susan Quinnell

Eric Gill: Nuptials of God
by Anthony Hoyland

*The Erotic Object: Sexuality in Sculpture
From Prehistory to the Present Day*
by Susan Quinnell

Minimal Art and Artists in the 1960s and After
by Laura Garrard

Land Art, Earthworks, Installations, Environments, Sculpture
by William Malpas

*Land Art: A Complete Guide to Landscape, Environmental,
Earthworks, Nature, Sculpture and Installation Art*
by William Malpas

Land Art In Close-Up
by William Malpas

*Colourfield Painting: Minimal, Cool, Hard Edge, Serial
and Post-Painterly Abstract Art From the Sixties to the Present*
by Laura Garrard

Mark Rothko: The Art of Transcendence
by Julia Davis

Jasper Johns
by L.M. Poole

BRICE MARDEN

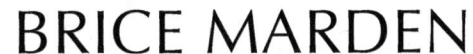

Brice Marden

Laura Garrard

CRESCENT MOON

First published 1994. Second edition 2007. Fourth edition 2012.
© Laura Garrard 2007, 2012.

Printed and bound in the U.S.A.
Set in Gill Sans 10 on 14pt.
Designed by Radiance Graphics.

British Library Cataloguing in Publication data

Garrard, Laura
Brice Marden
I. Title
759.13

ISBN-13 9781861713766 (Pbk)

ISBN-13 9781861713278 (Hbk)

CRESCENT MOON PUBLISHING
P.O. Box 1312, Maidstone,
Kent, ME14 5XU
Great Britain
www.crmoon.com

Contents

Acknowledgements

Thanks to Mirabelle Marden.

Thanks to Matthew Marks Gallery, New York, and Harry N. Abrams, publishers, New York and London.

Thanks to Karen, for first introducing me to Brice Marden's work.

Thanks to the authors quoted and their publishers, and to copyright owners of the illustrations.

Abbreviations

Look into that closed room, the empty chamber where brightness is born! Fortune and blessing gather where there is stillness.

Chuang-tzu

Some artists who have inspired Brice Marden (this page and over)

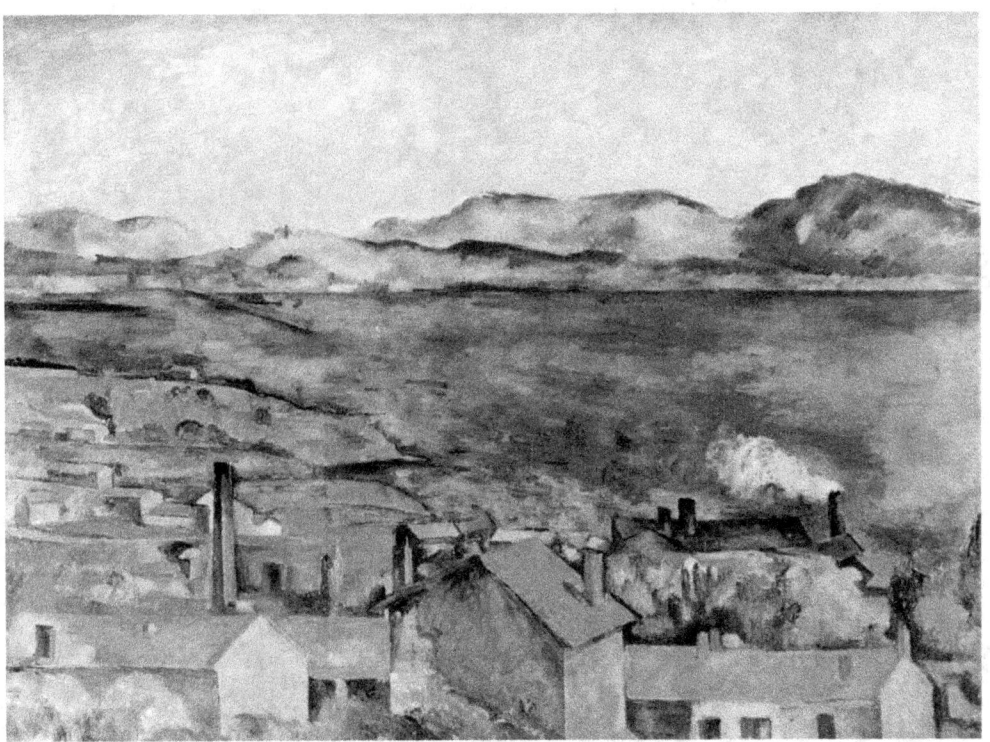

Paul Cézanne, The Bay From L'Estaque, c. 1886, Chicago

Diego de Velásquez, Juan de Pareja, 1650,
Metropolitan Museum of Art, New York

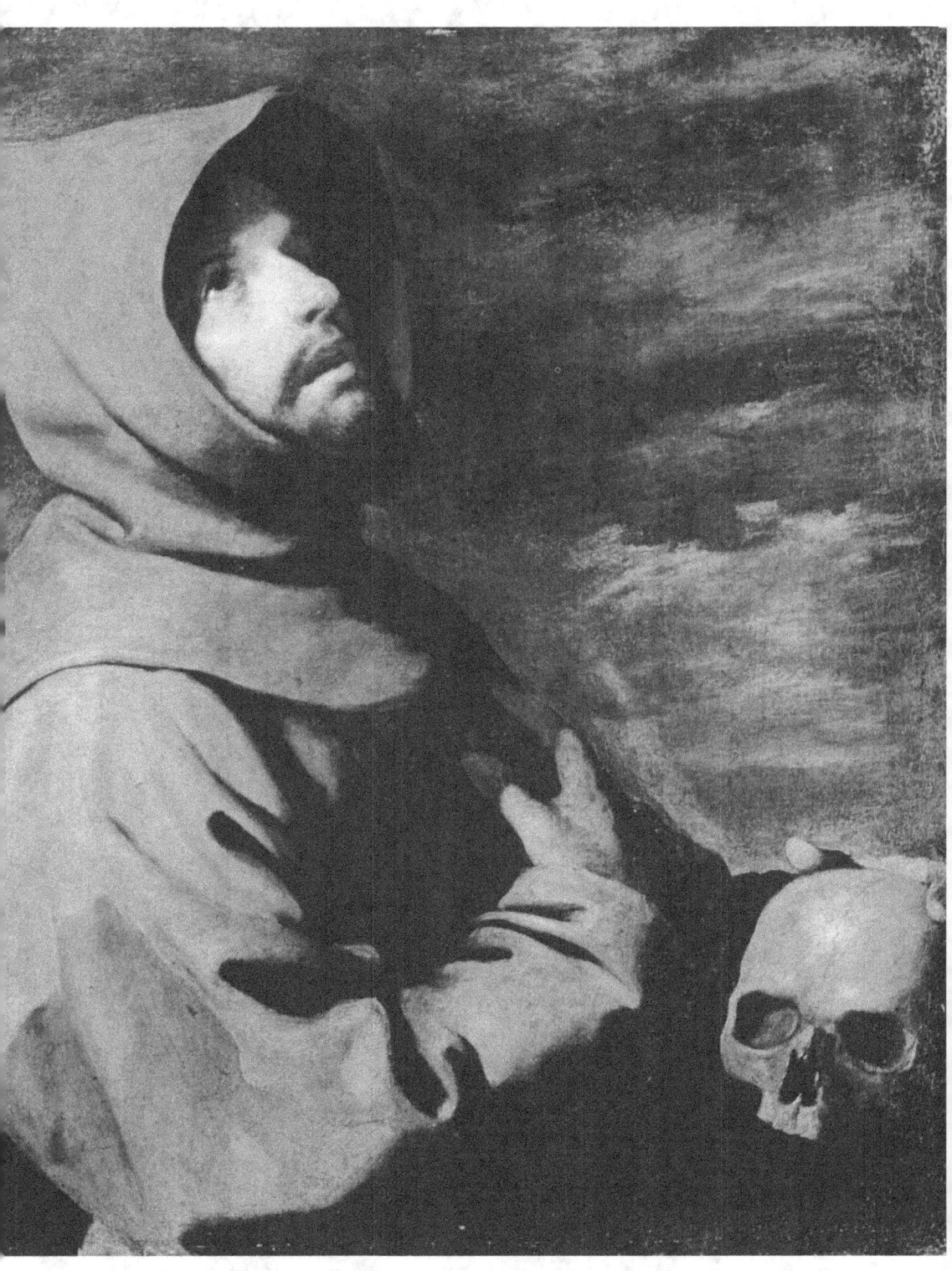

Francisco de Zurbarán, St Francis, Munich

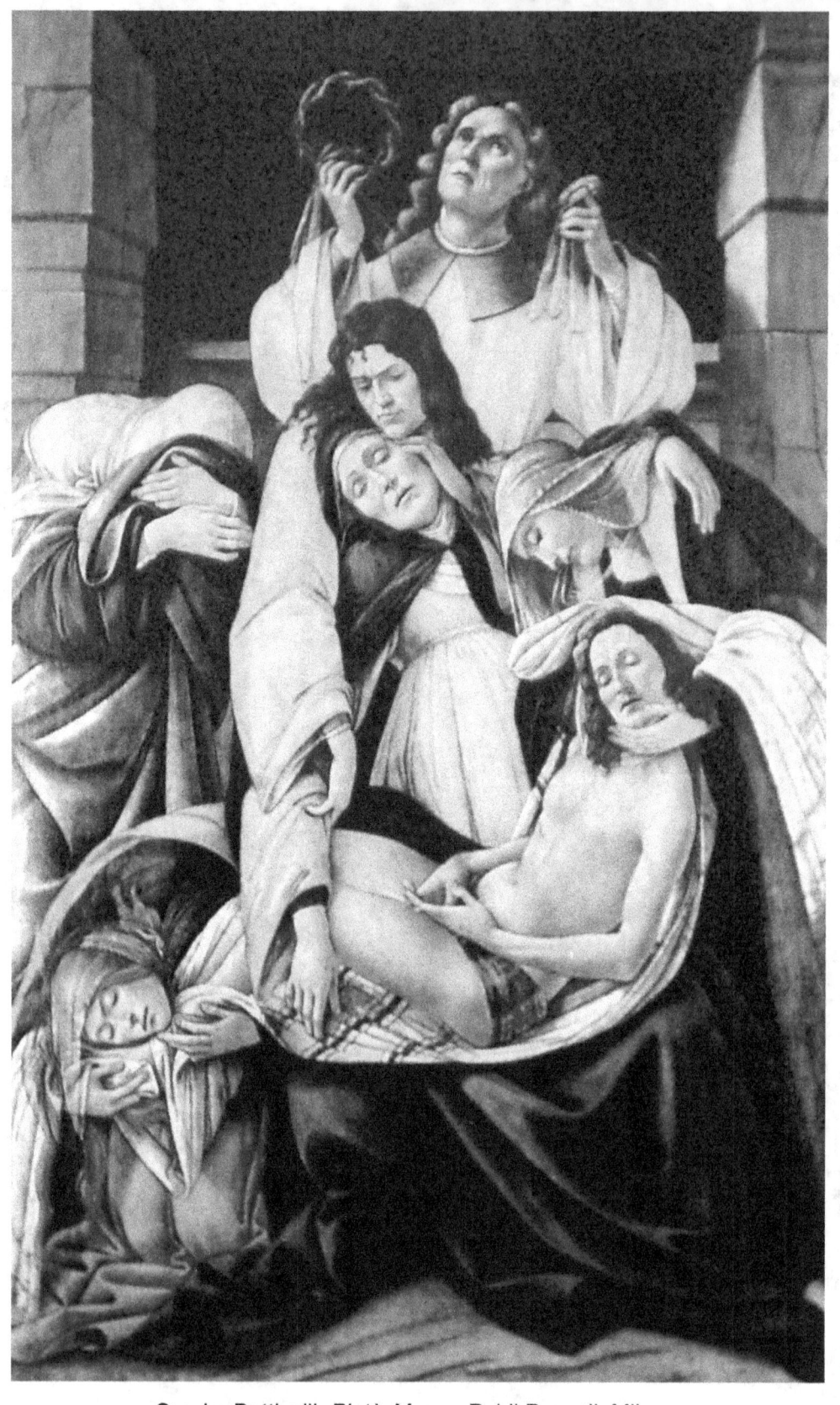

Sandro Botticelli, *Pietà*, Museo Poldi Pezzoli, Milan

CHAPTER *1*

Introduction to Brice Marden

BRICE MARDEN (born October 15, 1938, Bronxville, New York) is one of the foremost abstract painters of the late 20th century and beyond. He studied at Florida Southern College, Lakeland, and Boston University School of Fine and Applied Arts, receiving a Bachelor of Fine Arts in 1961. In 1961 he worked at Yale Norfolk Summer School in Connecticut. In 1963 he was awarded a Master of Fine Arts degree in painting from Yale University at New Haven. He moved to New York City, and worked as a guard in the Jewish Museum. At this time he was married to Pauline Baez, the sister of Joan Baez, the singer, and had a son, Nicholas (who was involved in the New York punk rock scene). Marden's second marriage was to Helen Harrington; they had two daughters, Mirabelle and Melia. Harrington appears a good deal in Marden's art.

In the mid-1960s Brice Marden began to have one-man exhibitions (typically at Bykert Gallery, where he had many shows). In 1966 he became an assistant to Robert Rauschenberg. In the late 1960s he started making multi-panel paintings. He worked as a painting instructor at the School of Visual Arts in New York from 1969-74. He had one-man shows and group shows in Europe (Milan, Turin, Paris, Düsseldorf). In 1975 there was a ten-year retrospective at the Guggenheim in New York, unusual for so young an artist (he was 37). From 1973 he visited Greece every year. Other major shows included a one-man exhibition of drawings (1964-74) at Contemporary Arts Museum, a drawing retrospective at Kunstraum Munich (1979), and the Whitechapel and Stedelijk Museum, Amsterdam one-man shows of 1981. An exhibition of prints 1961-91 travelled to the Tate Gallery, London, Baltimore Museum of Art and the Musée d'art moderne de la ville de Paris in 1992.

More recent exhibitions by Brice Marden include: *Brice Marden: Work of the 90s,* which travelled in 1999 to D.C., Dallas, Miami and Pittsburgh. *Brice Marden: Etchings* showed in L.A. in 2000; a retrospective of drawings was exhibited in Virginia in 2001; *Brice Marden: Attendants, Bears, and Rocks* appeared at Marden's regular New York gallery, Matthew Marks, in 2002 (with other solo shows in Boston and Rome in 2002; Marden exhibits often in Boston); group shows in 2003; group shows in 2004 included: *Matisse To Freud* (London), *Singular Forms* (Guggenheim), *A Minimal Future?* (Los Angeles), and *From Pollock To Marden* (Aspen); *Minimalism* and *Elemental Form* in 2006; a solo show in Boston (2007); a Boston alumni show in 2010; early 1960s paintings in Gotham in 2010; and *Brice Marden: Letters* in 2011 in NYC.

☆

Brice Marden's art combines elements from paganism and Christianity, nature and abstraction, Renaissance and contemporary art. Marden's art mixes the Old Master painterly traditions of Diego Velásquez, Francisco de Zurbarán, Édouard Manet and Paul Cézanne (L. Shearer, 1975, 10) with the contemporary art of Jasper Johns, Mark Rothko, Barnett Newman, Donald Judd and Frank Stella. It was 'very, very important', Marden reflected, that reproductions of Giovanni Bellini, Hans Holbein, Pablo Picasso and Rembrandt van Rijn were hung around his childhood home (M. Poirier, 1985, 54). Marden made a number of homages to various painters, in his **Homage to Art** and other groups of works. The **Homage to Art** works are collages founded on postcards of Old Master paintings. Around the postcards Marden added elements of graphite and beeswax. **Homage to Art 7 (Crucifixion)** (1973, collection: the artist) featured Diego Velásquez's stark **Crucifixion** (Prado in Madrid), in which Christ is seen against blackness; **Homage to Art 14** (1974, private collection) included three of the same postcards of a Renaissance angel; other homages included Piet Mondrian, Francisco de Goya, Francisco de Zurbarán and others.

Brice Marden writes of Francisco de Zurbarán: 'I like to read his paintings as very coldly executed yet very passionate.' (ib., 54) Similar dualities are at work in Marden's own paintings, which critics and viewers have seen as impenetrable and cold, yet they are clearly 'about' passionate, subjective experiences, from the experience of nature, the sea and the elements, to meditations on the Crucifixion and death. Marden's surfaces take time to open up and reveal themselves. The first perceptions of emptiness and denial of physicality give way to a formal (spiritual) richness and palpable physical presence. The dense planar geometry loses its initial reductive impenetrability, and depth is soon asserted. Denial becomes affirmation, and self-erasure becomes self (and world) glorification.

Like artists such as Frank Stella, Carl Andre and Donald Judd, Brice Marden has always made abstract art. There was no period of figurative work, as with the Abstract Expressionists, Mark Rothko, Jackson Pollock, Willem de Kooning and Robert Motherwell. They all drew and painted figurative art, much of it influenced by the Surrealists, before they turned to abstraction. Stella and Marden, though, were abstract artists from the beginning (although there are one or two early figurative works by Marden). Marden's art draws on Abstract Expressionism, however: he did not reject it as much as did Stella, Donald Judd and other Minimal artists. Marden speaks of the relation between himself and the two movements with which he is often associated, Abstract Expressionism and Minimalism:

> Rothko was talking about painting, about death and I was much more interested in that than in Judd's Minimalist æsthetic. Emotions? I wanted to keep that open. Subject matter was no longer valid but I felt my work was much more of a continuation of Abstract Expressionism than a rejection of it. (P, 55)

Although Barnett Newman's form of painting seems much more in tune with 1960s Minimalism than Mark Rothko's 'tragic' and 'transcendent' art, Brice Marden came to admire Rothko. In the mural series (especially in the 'Rothko Chapel' at Houston), Rothko had refined his sense of color and form radically, aligning it with the Christian Passion. Marden visited the Rothko Chapel in 1972, and the solemn, massive panels of color made a deep impression upon him (PD, 24). Later in the 1970s, Marden created his own series of religious abstract panels, the **Annunciation Series**. Interestingly, while Rothko moved through different phases from pseudo-figuration (in his post-Surrealist period), through the intense subjective expressionism of the radiantly colorful 1950s 'clouds' or 'things', to the radicalization of the dark, sombre, maroon murals series (the Seagram, Harvard and Houston paintings), Marden went the opposite way: beginning very austere and monotone, all in greys, in the 1960s, Marden opened up, relaxing into colorful reds, yellows and blues in his multi-canvas paintings of the 1970s, and branching out (literally – he used twigs to draw), into the 'calligraphic' drawings/ paintings of the 1980s and 1990s. For a time, in the late 1960s, Marden and Rothko were both making ascetic grey-on-grey abstract rectangular paintings. Rothko's dual-tone vertical grey rectangles were associated (by critics) with a cosmic, tragic exhaustion – the works presaged Rothko's suicide in 1970. Marden's Minimalist grey horizontal rectangles, meanwhile, were associated with personal depression, alienation from his wife, the *ennui* of a young artist searching for his voice.

What is striking about Brice Marden's education and career is how academic and historically-aware it is. He was highly trained in art history and the practice of painting, as the Bachelor and Master of Fine Art degrees show. He spent a lot of time in colleges and universities of one sort of another – Boston University, Florida Southern College, New York School of Visual Arts. Some of these, such as Yale University, were the key educational establishments in North America. Fellow students at Yale included the extraordinary sculptor Nancy Graves, Superrealist Chuck Close, the abstract painter Robert Mangold, and the influential sculptor Richard Serra, whose metal leaning slabs were one of the most distinctive products of 1960s Minimalism.

Brice Marden has been part of the mainstream international art world for a long time: he has been associated with the prestigious institutions of the art world: Kassel (1972), Guggenheim (1975), the Whitney Biennial (1977), Stedelijk (1981), and Royal Academy (1981). His jobs as a guard at the Jewish Museum and as assistant to the larger-than-life Robert Rauschenberg must have influenced his work. As a museum guard, for instance, Marden would have had endless hours to contemplate the work on display. At the Jewish Museum he admired Jasper Johns' work, in retrospective, in particular Johns' grey paintings, such as **Gray Numbers**. Grey became one of Marden's (and Minimalism's) key colors of the mid-1960s. The influence of Jasper Johns is explored below, in the chapters on oil and wax and Minimalism. Robert Rauschenberg's influence on Marden is harder to spot than Johns' quiet intensity: Rauschenberg is an extraordinarily dynamic artist, whose work displays an energetic exploration of painterly possibilities. Rauschenberg had, for example, painted all-white paintings years before 1960s Minimalism (in 1951). Interestingly, one of Marden's jobs when he worked for Rauschenberg was to repaint the white paintings as they yellowed with age (J. Taylor, 1976, 66).

CHAPTER *2*

Romantic Presence:
Brice Marden and
the Abstract Expressionists

BRICE MARDEN is a painter who follows on directly from the Abstract Expressionists, in particular that form of heroic Abstract Expressionism (called the 'Abstract Sublime' or 'heroic' abstraction) as produced by Mark Rothko and Barnett Newman. As with Rothko and Newman, Marden's art evokes Romanticism, humane emotions, mystery, ambiguity, tradition, history and presence. In painters such as Franz Kline and Ad Reinhardt, Marden appreciated a committment to severely reduced color (in particular black and white). Marden made a series of drawings based on one of Kline's paintings (*Zinc Door*, 1961) while he was still at Yale. Kline was important, too, in leading Marden towards painters who had mastered the use of black (such as Francisco de Zurbarán, Diego Velásquez and Édouard Manet). Marden rejected some of the grand gestures of Abstract Expressionism, particularly the heavily gestural painting of Willem de Kooning and Franz Kline. Marden saw some of the gestures of the second wave Abstract Expressionists (one thinks of Kline and Robert Motherwell) as too clichéd. But, unlike many Minimal artists who reacted against the 'excesses of deep subjectivity and allusive emotionalism'[1] of Abstract Expressionism, Marden moved towards those economies more and more.

Brice Marden seems closer to Barnett Newman than Mark Rothko. One can see a direct strain of painting moving from Newman's 'all-over' paintings to Marden's monochrome panels. Newman's form of Abstract Expressionism is an obvious precursor of Minimalism, and of Marden's 1960s one-color paintings. Newman said: 'I was concerned constantly in doing a painting that would move in its totality as you see it. You look at it and you see it.' (E. De Antonio, 70) Frank Stella writes thus of Barnett Newman, and of Morris Louis, and much of what he says applies to Brice Marden:

> The strength of his [Newman's] painting comes from the ability of the stripes (or, as he liked to call them, "zips") to attach themselves to and into the background. They fit beautifully, zipping the space together. Newman sets up the motion of his figuration counter to the motion of the space supporting it... It may be that what makes Morris Louis's late paintings so appealing is their peculiar Kandinsky-like understanding of Newman. Louis brought a determined looseness to Newman's abstraction that Kandinsky would have applauded. Louis had the opportune sense of contiguous touch that is so necessary to link the moving elements of abstraction. This touch enabled him to exploit separation in a way that modern painting admires but cannot seem to imitate. [2]

And Frank Stella may be thinking of Brice Marden's type of painterly abstraction when he writes in **Working Space**:

> The limited, difficult space of Kandinsky, Malevich, Mondrian, Pollock, and Newman has degenerated into the self-effacing, almost non-pictorial space of 1970s abstraction. Recent painting appears to have resolved spatial problems in such a way that various unruly elements, such as the boxy depth of Cubism, the constricted linearity of nonobjective painting, and the optical flatness of hard-edge painting, have been tidied up by a burst of illustrative superficiality. The result is an easy-to-read, inert space, refined by a heavily pigmented surface and cropped to convenient but often intensely a-pictorial shapes. As if this were not enough, whatever spatial vitality is left is rendered oppressively dull by the application of close-valued color.[3]

One senses a thinly-veiled vehemence behind Frank Stella's attack on post-1970 abstraction. Stella's indictment of this form of abstraction is similar to other critical reactions that Brice Marden's 1960s and 1970s paintings engender. Stella too regards 1970 as a key moment in the history of abstract painting, for here Post-Painterly Abstraction had run its course, had 'turned to ashes' (1986, 1). For Stella, post-1970 abstract painting was/ is full of dull, flat, shallow acrylic surfaces: 'unbearably thin and shallow' (1986, 42-43). Worse, abstract painting, Stella maintains, 'has always been flawed by spatial conservatism.' (1986, 43) This statement seems odd, when so many people seem to have problems even now with abstract painting, as if abstract painting were too 'avant garde', too 'mod', too 'difficult'. No, says, Stella, abstraction is not *avant garde*, it is conservative. For Stella, abstract art 'has rendered itself space-blind' in order to survive, because to survive art must become literary (1986, 46). Certainly, if Stella's view of post-1970 painting is applied to Marden's art, it does ring true. Marden's work is 'literary', in its mythic allusions, for instance; Marden's work is 'flat, dull, inert', to use Stella's terms (criticisms which are often levelled against Marden).

CHAPTER *3*

The Art of Brice Marden

SURFACE
◆

THE SENSUALITY of surfaces, of textures, of brushwork, of the artist's
sense of touch, so central to Brice Marden's work, is crucial to the
'greatness' of art, as Lynda Nead writes: 'the artist's subjectivity
that is registered by the brushwork and surface is sexualized. Art
criticism writes sex into descriptions of paint, surface and forms.'
(58) Paul Gauguin wrote of the sensual primacy of painting in the
familiar terms of late 19th century Baudelairean 'theory of correspondences', which was used by many poets, painters and
dramatists:

> *Painting is the most beautiful of all arts. In it, all sensations are*
> *condensed... A complete art which sums up all the others and completes*
> *them. – Like music, it acts on the soul through the intermediary senses:*

harmonious colors correspond to the harmonies of sounds. [1]

The **jouissance** or eroticism of abstract painting is obvious to those who find surfaces erotic. Other artists have spoken lovingly of the loving nature of the canvas itself, the beauty of the art object. Maurice Denis wrote: '[t]he emotion – bitter or sweet, "literary" as the painters say – emerges from the canvas itself, a plane surface covered with colors.'[2] Paintings create worlds, worlds, if they are successful, which involve the viewer. The good painting extends well beyond the painting. The sense of space in an artwork is crucial for Jasper Johns too:

> *As well as I can tell, I am concerned with space. With some idea about space. And then as soon as you break space, then you have things'*[3]

Max Kozloff wrote in 1962 of Jasper Johns' motifs, the flags and targets saying they were

> *merely so many abstract forms upon which social usage has conferred meaning, but which now, displaced into their new context, cease to function socially. From this tremendous insight alone have sprung the momentum of Pop Art and the huge quantities of abstraction that is emblematic in character.*[4]

The key to Jasper Johns' reworking of formalism and abstraction in the flags, targets, numbers and alphabets was precisely the sensuality of his art. In this Brice Marden's 1960s and 1970s canvases partake of the same paradox: apparent flatness and non-figuration combined with intense sensuality.

It was the way Jasper Johns and Brice Marden so powerfully employed the techniques of the Old Masters, of 'great art', that made their works so successful. Critics could not see Johns' banal signs culled from popular culture as trivial art, for Johns, like Marden, used one of the key elements in high art: the sensual, heavily impastoed surface. Johns' art could not be dismissed by critics, then as now, because its surface is as sensual and painterly as Rembrandt van Rijn, Diego Velásquez, Édouard Manet or Titian.

OIL AND WAX
◆

The sensitivity of response with the materials, in particular oil and wax, is crucial for Brice Marden's painting. The parallels between Brice Marden and Jasper Johns are again enlightening here. Johns used to become totally absorbed in his painted surfaces. What a critic wrote of Johns' painterly absorption might apply also to Marden:

> He lives in those surfaces. The surfaces are his whole world, they are everything. He loses himself in them. They are everything.[5]

Jasper Johns' tactile surfaces were built up using wax – the thick impasto of oil and wax is one of the keys to his textures, for when the wax cools, you can paint on top of it very soon, instead of waiting for the paint to dry.[6] Johns used encaustic and oil because he wanted evidence of the gestures he made **before** and **after**, that is, a finished painting which would reveal its making. It is these seemingly simple and obvious techniques and stratagems that concern artists, this dealing with such simple but important processes such as drying paint. Tony Godfrey writes of Marden's use of oil and wax:

> He worked his paintings in a series of layers of oil and wax and turpentine that seemed to capture extraordinarily precise sensations of color and light, while their materiality was as exposed as Kiefer's or Rauschenberg's. (124)

Brice Marden draws on Jasper Johns' oil and wax technique, but he is not particularly interested in keeping the expressive gestural paintwork of Johns. Marden favours a flattened brush style, like Barnett Newman, so that individual brush strokes cannot be seen over most of the paint surface. Marden's oil and wax paintings have a uniform paint surface, which is opaque and smooth. The wax is kept warm and mixed in small quantities with the paint (Marden used a refrigerator door as a palette). The aim is to keep the surfaces in a painting 'constant and total' ("Technical Statement", G, 28), typical Minimal sentiments. Marden sometimes applied paint with a spatula after using a brush, to achieve a smoothness. There are no gestural marks, as in Johns' flags and targets. At the same time, the sense of color does not rest entirely on the surface; like Mark Rothko's paintings, Marden's canvases suggest layering, with colors underneath leaving ghostly traces on the surfaces. Not all art critics saw the underlying colors and gauzes of paint: Scott Burton wrote of Marden's Bykert Gallery show of 1966 that Marden's colors were 'closed', like skin: 'you can't look into them, only at them.'[7]

Brice Marden works on one panel until he has attained the right kind of color value. Then he moves onto another panel, building that one up until it has the correct color values: it is the relationship between the two that interests him. With three panels, the process is more complex. Sometimes the paintings work quickly, sometimes it takes hours to get the right effects. The painter is 'always going back and forth' (1978, W, 55), making colors darker or lighter as required, often with much repainting. When there is a lot of reworking, the oil and wax becomes so thick it gives the paint surface a texture that is waxy, that is like skin. The weave of the cotton duck canvas can no longer be seen: the surface becomes more opaque and intense. Marden works in a dialogue with his paintings, as most artists do: they talk to him as much as he expresses himself through them (1973, W, 55). The slowness of the paintings' manufacture, Linda Shearer suggests in 1975 (G, 12), adds to the slowness of the perceptual response: they take so long to produce, they really require a long time to be fully perceived.

It is interesting to compare Brice Marden's painterly technique with his contemporary, Kenneth Noland, who said:

> Sometimes I apply the paint with brushes, sometimes with rollers... any way that I can get it on where the tactile result is compatible with the nature of the color I'm going to use there... When the color is first laid down, it doesn't have anything to do with the resulting size or shape really. Once you lay it down, you can choose by sight how to bring the total color into a certain quantity... For instance, I could make that picture more square, and if I made it more square, then it would become denser and the color would have movement in it. If I extended it longer, you would have a faster kind of movement. You have a way of getting the color to take on a different degree of speed, translucence, transparency, opacity, density, even to the warmth or coolness for that matter. (in E. De Antonio, 84)

COLOUR
◆

Brice Marden's sense of color and abstraction draws largely on the Old Masters, the Spanish masters, and Northern European painting. Robert Rosenblum, in his influential book **Modern Painting and the Northern Romantic Tradition** , saw Northern European painters as being the precursors of modern abstraction, and the masters of modern abstract art – Piet Mondrian, Wassily Kandinsky, Kasimir Malevich, Paul Klee – are distinctly Northern European figures. Marden sees himself as a Northern painter (M. Poirier, 52), and his paintings, especially the ones of the late 1960s and early 1970s, have the austerity and mystery of Northern European painters such as Caspar Friedrich, Emil Nolde and Malevich. The spiritual discourse of the modern abstract artists (the affinities with Rudolf Steiner, theosophy, occultism, Rosicrucianism, Qabbalism, etc), is a key element in the art of Malevich, Kandinsky, Mondrian and Klee. This European taste for the sublime and mystical was later developed by the Abstract Expressionists (the *Qabbalah* in Barnett Newman, Judæo-Christianity in Rothko, Zen Buddhism in Ad Reinhardt, Robert Motherwell and Franz Kline), and in Brice Marden we find Classical mythology, sacred architecture, the Christian Annunciation, the symbolism of numbers (numerology), alchemy, and so on. While fellow 1960s artists rejected such spiritual hankerings (Frank Stella, Donald Judd, Dan Flavin, Roberts Morris and Mangold, Richard Serra and Kenneth Noland), Marden embraced them (as did, in their own way, Carl Andre, David Novros, Eva Hesse, Ad Reinhardt and Morris Louis).

PHYSICALITY
◆

The 1960s was an era which drew attention to the **physicality** of artworks. Color was another element in the physicality of an art object. Color was treated in the same physical way as the other formal aspects of the artwork (size, shape, texture, weight, etc). For the Post-Painterly Abstractionists (Morris Louis, Frank Stella, Jules Olitski, Ellsworth Kelly, Richard Diebenkorn and Marcia Hafif), color has a direct sensual effect. The symbolic and iconological aspects of color were seen as not as important as haptic physicality. Kenneth Noland spoke of the physicality of color:

> One thing that people don't generally talk about is the fact that the experience of color is tactile. We talk about the relative coolness and warmness of color, or transparency or opacity, and really all those descriptive terms are tactile descriptions rather than to do with the redness of red. (K. Noland, in E. De Antonio, 84)

For a long time, Brice Marden's colors were extremely subdued. Though we speak of Marden in the same breath as Kenneth Noland, Frank Stella, Ellsworth Kelly and Jules Olitski, Marden's 1960s colors were nowhere near as brilliant and saturated as theirs. Compare a canvas by Olitski, Noland or Kelly with one by Marden and you see bright greens, radiant yellows and pulsating scarlets in the former, while Marden's canvases sink deep into grey, light brown, beige, and more grey. For Minimal sculptors, grey, white and black were suitably 'neutral' colors which did not scream expressively, as reds and purples had done in the work of Mark Rothko or Willem de Kooning. It was years, really – until the mid-1970s – before Marden used colors as glowing as the Post-Painterly Abstractionists.

FLATNESS
◆

Brice Marden's paintings, like those of Morris Louis, Frank Stella, Robert Mangold, Agnes Martin and Robert Ryman, were not concerned with creating 'illusionistic space', with the space of traditional Western post-Renaissance art, but with a new flatness. Early Stella attested the flatness of painting. His famous statement runs thus:

> *My painting is based on the fact that only what can be seen there is there... What you see is what you see.*[8]

Clement Greenberg had noted that any painterly mark alters the state of the canvas: '[t]he first mark made on a canvas destroys the literal and utter flatness', he wrote.[9] Jackson Pollock had moved in this direction with his 'non-figurative' skeins of color.[11] But when you come upon Brice Marden, Kenneth Noland, Morris Louis and Frank Stella you see the paint straight on the canvas, with no attempts at the usual forms of traditional Renaissance illusion, other than a simple pattern. When you first confront a Minimal painting, and see the bare canvas, it stops you up short. Something is different about Minimal paintings. You don't at first notice what it is. You look closer: yes, you can see raw canvas. This bare canvas is not a sly reference on the painter's part to the manufacture of the painting (though it is that too). They are not showing the canvas to show you how the painting is made, much as a movie camera can pull back from a scene to show the lights, crew, director and people standing around bored and smoking. Marden, Noland, Louis and Stella reveal the canvas for different reasons. The paint on their canvases is not 'representational', in the usual sense. It is not paintwork referring to something outside of itself. It is there, it partakes of **thereness** or **dasein**, to use the terms of Zen Buddhism and Existentialism, two important influences on postwar American art. Rainer Maria Rilke spoke of the 'thereness' of things, 'Kunst-Ding' he called it.

A new sort of painting is created. For Sheldon Nodelman, Frank Stella and Kenneth Noland created a new fusion of paint and canvas, so that 'no contrast' will be 'set up between the image-content and the picture-object'.[11] Finally, a painting will become an object, as Jo Baer writes:

> The last radical paintings to attend to figure-ground problems were Noland's circle paintings of about 1960. Painters discarded ground altogether, and paintings became objects altogether.[12]

On the other side of the flat painting camp, there were artists whose aim was to destroy the rigid flatness of painting. One painter who threw anything onto the picture plane was Robert Rauschenberg (see his many 'combine' paintings, those mixed media extravaganzas). Claes Oldenburg's soft telephones and toilets far outdo Rauschenberg for pure silliness. Oldenburg like Andy Warhol questioned the holy notion of 'Art' with a capital 'A'. The picture plane, which had been so scrupulously flat throughout the Renaissance (ignoring the embossed and punched gold), suddenly burst open in contemporary art. As Clement Greenberg put it: '[p]ictorial space has lost its "inside" and become all "outside".'[13] Of course, some postwar artists asserted the flatness of the picture plane even more fervently: Morris Louis with his stained, furled canvas, Frank Stella with his black stripes done with housepaint direct onto cotton duck, Mark Rothko with his cloud-like shapes, Agnes Martin with her finely pencilled squares, and Sol LeWitt with his spacious wall-drawings. Lucio Fontana, though, destroyed the flatness of the canvas in a phallic, penetrative fashion: he slashed the canvas. Fontana explained his seemingly violent, nay, pornographic act thus:

> I want to open up space, create a new dimension for art, tie in at the cosmos as it endlessly expands beyond the confining place of the picture. With my innovation of the hole pierced through the canvas in repetitive perforations, I have not attempted to decorate a surface, but, on the contrary, I have tried to break its dimensional limitations. Beyond the perforations a newly gained freedom of interpretation awaits us, but also, and just as inevitably, the end of art.[14]

Brice Marden too spoke of wanting to 'go beyond' (referring to Francisco de Zurbarán). He was looking for an 'art in extremis' (1989, in PD, 15).

ABSTRACTION AND NATURE
◆

'I paint nature,' says Brice Marden. 'I mean, I refer to nature... it's what the painting is about.' (1980, W, 57) Marden's æsthetics have more to do with the Abstract Expressionists than the Minimal artists, who did not refer to nature in the same subjective, emotional way. For Marden, painting (art) is emotional, about expression and essence. Marden believed that his paintings were 'highly emotional', made in a 'highly subjective state', albeit within strict limits (1963, W, 54). These notions are diametrically opposed to the flattening seriality of Minimalism, which usually studiously avoids sentimentality. Increasingly, Marden referred to nature, or, rather, he made the references to nature more explicit (R. White, 1980). Nature had always been there. Many paintings refer to specific places, for the 'spirit of place' the **deus loci**, has always been important to Marden. **Sea Painting, Moon, Hydra, Thira, Grove Group, Toward Brindisi, To Corfu, Seasons, Nebraska Range** – these are paintings which directly refer to nature, even if, in their non-figurative oceans of oil and wax, it is sometimes difficult to detect nature.

THE BODY
◆

Brice Marden's paintings refer directly to the body in their scale and proportion and size. They are 'human' scale paintings, as if paintings could have any other scale than 'human'. Anything made by humans must relate in some way or another to humans. Marden's paintings are not too large as to be overwhelming, like Mark Rothko's or Morris Louis' enormous canvases. They are not intended to be dwarfing like some French history paintings (Charles LeBrun, for example). Marden's paintings are not small works, either, like, say, Howard Hodgkin's, or Jasper Johns' **Flags**. The scale of Marden's paintings is restrained but also self-assured; not large and brash but not small and insignificant either. A painting such as **The Dylan Karina Painting** is large – 96 by 144 inches – but it is more typical of Marden's canvases to be between 60 and 84 inches high. Indeed, six feet is a favourite size, as is 84 inches. These sizes – six and seven feet – are tall enough to enable the paintings to assert themselves authoritatively before the viewer, but not too large to be over-powering. Yet Mark Rothko's large scale was, he said, in order to promote intimacy. This, too, is what Marden wishes to produce, an intimate contact between viewer and artwork.

Brice Marden's **Back Series** was based directly on the human figure (in this case, Marden's wife, Helen Harrington,). In the **Back** paintings Marden celebrated the human figure in his usual severely formal, abstract terms which nevertheless used the traditional devices of art. For example, on the announcement for the Bykert Gallery show of the **Back Series** paintings in January 1968, there was a photograph taken in the artist's studio of Marden's wife, standing nude in front of his paintings. The female nude situated in the artist's studio is one of the archetypal images of European art (Egon Schiele, Gustave Courbet, Jean Auguste Dominique Ingres, etc). Marden's nine **Back Series** take their proportions from Helen Marden's body: the paintings are all 69 inches high, her height (their width, 45 inches, is an intuitive dimension). In the **Back Series** and later works (such as the ones in the 1972 Bykert Gallery show), Marden conflated life and art in the age-old manner of traditional (Western) art. Equivalents were inferred between: women and art; the nude woman and the painting; skin and paint surface. The **Back Series** can be seen as Muse paintings, as homages to Marden's wife, as paintings which contain, dare we use the word, love. Helen Marden was indeed an important person for Marden: she discovered some of the key sacred places of his work, notably Greece and Hydra.

During the making of the **Annunciation Series** (1977-8), Helen Marden was pregnant with Mirabelle, their first daughter, which may have been significant, as the **Annunciation Paintings** were all about the holiness of conception, pregnancy, birth and mother-hood – in a word, 'feminine' mysteries. Brice Marden is actually one of the few major artists to acknowledge the value of his lover in his art. Hundreds of other artists' wives and lovers have gone unsung, even though they were sometimes enormously influential. Maybe the exaltation of Helen Harrington in Marden's **Back Series** is not that great after all: she is shown in the studio photo looking down, arms folded defensively over her chest, looking dejected. And Marden's stark monochrome paintings with their 'unnameable'[15] colors and 'nearly unseeable textures and their diffident beeswax gleam'[16] might not be everyone's idea of celebration. Indeed, some critics saw them as funerary artifacts, abstract tombstones painted in order to 'stave off the death of painting by celebrating it in advance with such solemn, occasion-ally sullen flair' (C. Ratcliff, ib.). While it was common in the early 1960s to hear the ponderous judgement that 'painting is dead', Marden himself never believed it.[18]

For Helen (1967) is a happier painting, one of the first vertical multi-panel works (related to **Pair,** 1965). In **For Helen** the two narrow panels are quite wide apart (for a Brice Marden multi-panel work): two inches apart. The gap between the two panels creates a strip which recalls Barnett Newman's zip. **Pair** was a small (18" x 38") diptych which, unusually for Marden, employed the square. The pale white/ light grey tones of **Pair**, **Return I** (1964-5) and other early works recalls the white paintings of Roberts

Rauschenberg and Ryman (especially in **Return I**, which is not painted smoothly, like later Marden monochromes). Other paintings which referred to people included **The Dylan Painting, Star** (for Patti Smith), **For Pearl, T.K.B., For Otis, For Me, Private Title, Three Deliberate Grays For Jasper Johns, For Carl Andre, Nico's Painting** and **4:1 (for David Novros).**

CHAPTER *4*

Brice Marden and Minimal Art

MUCH OF Minimal philosophy can be traced to statements such as this famous one by Jasper Johns:1

Take an object
Do something to it
Do something else to it
" " " "

Brice Marden took up the Minimal notion of seriality and repetition (C. Ratcliff, 130), as did so many other artists in the 1960s, and explored it in monochrome canvas after canvas. For Jasper Johns the aim was to create 'things which are seen and not looked at', and he explained further:

Using the design of the American flag took care of a great deal for me
because I didn't have to design it. So I went on to similar things like the

❖ 43

*targets – things the mind already knows. That gave me room to work on
other levels.2*

Brice Marden employed the æsthetics of Minimalism in his
paintings: seriality, repetition, symmetry, flatness, abstraction,
functionalism, and monochrome, etc.

The great shape of the Minimal era was the cube, which was
found in David Smith's proto-Minimal sculpture, in Robert Morris,
in Donald Judd, in Sol LeWitt's hundreds of interconnected white
cubes. The Minimal cube was hard-edged, flat, precise, a mathe-
matically perfect environment. Brice Marden stuck to the rectangle, which was the fundamental shape of just about all his
drawings, prints and paintings. He spoke of 'that incredibly
intense rectangle', while in some notes for 1971/ 72, Marden
spoke about the spiritual dimension of the formal aspects of
painting: the rectangle, he suggested, like the plane and the structure, 'are but sounding for the spirit' (W, 54). Marden's paintings
explore the possibilities the rectangle offers, its scale, size, and
relationship to proportion, space, color and light. A rectangle is
not simply a thing static and fixed forever. As the Greeks knew,
there are certain rectangles that chime with the eyes and soul,
while other rectangles have different, sometimes negative
properties. In some paintings Marden breaks up the rectangle, and
has the dripped edge along the bottom of it (this device was
derived from Jasper Johns [L. Shearer, 12]). With that bare paint-
dripped edge, the rectangle re-organizes its internal proportions.

The other major Brice Marden form is the grid, which is
intimately related to the rectangle. Early works associated with the
grid included the paintings **Untitled** (1962-3) and **Return I**, and
the charcoal drawings **Untitled** (1965), **Untitled** (1964) and

Untitled (1962-3, PD, 145, 149, 150). In print after print, Marden explored the relation between an internal, drawn grid and the physical limits of the rectangle. He explored the relationships between the 'real', physical rectangle of the print or painting, and the 'imagined' rectangle. His art for years was always a matter of straight horizontal and vertical lines. The paintings were always constructed of rectangular panels, placed flush with each other, creating one large rectangle. Works such as **Thira** complexly interlinked rectangular canvas panels. Even two panels set beside each other could create complicated relationships between their size, their shape, the height above the floor, the distance from the wall, the perfection or otherwise of the join between them, and so on.

Brice Marden's rectangles seem to be part of the Hard-Edge painting type, as epitomized in Jack Youngerman, Kenneth Noland and Ellsworth Kelly. The edges of the painting and the shapes within it are not 'hard' in Marden's art, however. His edges, though they are always strictly rectangular, all exact straight lines, are soft, blurred.

☆

For Hilton Kramer, Abstract Expressionism was all about painting, about reducing painting to nothing more than painting that referred to its manufacture, to its essence, as a material object (E. De Antonio, 143). It was this materiality that Robert Rauschenberg liked about the Abstract Expressionists: 'they let their brushstrokes show', Rauschenberg said, there was a sense of materiality about their works (ib, 87). The Post-Painterly, post-Abstract Expressionist painters – Marden, Ellsworth Kelly, Kenneth Noland, Richard Diebenkorn, Morris Louis and Ad Reinhardt – are regarded by some critics as having squeezed out the emotion from painting: they took the Abstract Expressionist forms and made them unexpressive. Lawrence Alloway writes in "Residual Sign Systems in Abstract Expressionism":

> *If we compare paintings by Frank Stella and Ellsworth Kelly with those of the Abstract Expressionists, it becomes evident that a dimension of allusion, an aura of content, has been denied by the later artists. They certainly take off from positions given by Newman, Rothko, but the field of color, the holistic imagery, and the expanded scale of the canvas no longer imply momentous content. The allusions of older artists' feelings compared to the reduced passion of the younger generation...3*

There does not seem to be much going on in Brice Marden paintings, as in most Minimal paintings. But there is, in fact, a lot going on. Marden simply limits himself to a narrow set of rules. Like Kenneth Noland, Barnett Newman, Morris Louis and Mark Rothko, Marden sets himself to explore only a few configurations of painting. But these things – shape of the canvas, internal organization of the shapes, color of the rectangles – offer up endless permutations. Painters go over the same simple patterns and set-ups again and again. J.M.W. Turner painted thousands of seascapes – the same basic ocean, framed in the same lower third of the picture, the same mixture of clouds and sun in the sky, etc. Similarly, Claude Monet painted the same basic picture of a sunlit river time after time. Like other Minimal artists, Marden explored the endless permutations that a few very simple elements offered up. The results seem to be 'lean', but even in the most minimal of Minimalist works there is sensuality and presence. Samuel Wagstaff notes that the Minimalist painting asserts the painting above the painter: the author slips into the background: '[t]here is an attempt to suggest the presence of paint rather than the

presence of the painter.'[4] And Helen Frankenthaler said, like so
many 1960s painters, that she didn't want the manufacture of the
painting to be apparent: 'I poured the paint and used relatively
few brushstrokes. I didn't want the sign of the brush or how the
picture was made to appear.'[5] Helen Frankenthaler spoke of the
way a really good picture looks 'as if it all happened or was made
in one stroke at once.' (E. De Antonio, 85) This compares with
Barnett Newman's sense of all-overness and Zen Buddhist totality,
but Frankenthaler's sense of instantaneousness was intended to
hide the manufacture of the painting, something earlier Abstract
Expressionists – Jackson Pollock, Adolph Gottlieb, Clyfford Still –
were keen to keep prominent. Michael Fried said that the presence
of Frank Stella's paintings could not be 'understood solely in
terms of their physical and formal characteristics.'[7] Marden's
paintings are even leaner than Stella's, Noland's or Louis's, but
this æsthetic leanness does not necessarily mean unfeelingness.
This is the problem that monochrome painting creates, and
Minimal art in general. People think Minimal art is boring. In
Minimal painting and sculpture, surfaces are, typically, smooth,
utterly smooth and 'pure'. Simplicity is exalted, as is repetition,
seriality, process, and flatness (flatness but also volume and
space). The many materials are flattened out and depersonalized,
and gestures, so important to certain kinds of painting and
sculpture, such as that of Pablo Picasso or Michelangelo Buonarroti, are suppressed. Indeed, the flatness of the surfaces, whether
in the art of Robert Morris, Donald Judd, Agnes Martin, Carl
Andre, Tony Smith or Brice Marden, is crucial. But the 'boringness' of Minimal art[7] becomes a part of the metaphysics of
Minimal art, so that Lucy Lippard writes:

The exciting thing about… the "cool" artists is their daring challenge of

*the concepts of boredom, monotony and repetition... their demonstration
that intensity does not have to be melodramatic.* 8

Boring art for some is exhilarating art for others, just as erotic art
for some is pornography for others. Thus, James Mellow wrote
that one of Donald Judd's shows was 'one of the most provoc-
ative of the season'.9 On 'boringness', Robert Morris commented
that art is found 'boring' by those who desire 'specialness':

> *Such work which has the feel and look of openness, extendibility,
> accessibility, publicness, repeatability, equanimity, directness,
> immediacy, and has been formed by clear decision rather than groping
> craft would seem to have a few social implications, none of which are
> negative. Such work would undoubtedly be boring to those who long for
> access to an exclusive specialness, the experience of which reassures their
> superior perception.*10

Minimal artists such as Brice Marden, Donald Judd, Robert
Mangold, Sol LeWitt and Robert Morris explored the notions of
'boringness' and 'interestingness'. 'Boring art is interesting art',
noted Frances Colpitt in her book on Minimalism (121). Donald
Judd, the chief explicator of Minimal æsthetics, wrote: 'I can't see
how any good work can be boring or monotonous in the usual
sense of those words', adding: '[a]nd no one has developed an
unusual sense of them.'11

Clearly, the Minimal artists thought they were making
'interesting' art. Or at least, **they** were interested in it. If art's good,
it can't be 'boring', cliamed Donald Judd, claiming that 'a work
needs only to be interesting'. The discussion of 'interesting',
'boring' and 'value' becomes a quagmire of semantics and the
metaphysics of meaning. Language soon fails to describe the
kinds of intentions that artists have, and the kind of responses that
critics have to works. Robert Mangold said 'I certainly know

whether I'm interested in the work or whether I'm not interested
in the work.' (in F. Colpitt, 121) Sol LeWitt explained his view
thus:

> *I wouldn't say that I wanted to like uninteresting things or to dislike
> interesting things. I think that's one way that you measure your response,
> if it interests you. 'Interests' means that it somehow makes a bridge
> between you and it, you and the object, you and the art object. If it hits
> home, it means that it's of interest. (ib., 121)*

You might see Robert Ryman's white-on-white paintings as
unsensual, flat, 'boring'. In fact, Ryman's paintings are very
powerful. The surfaces themselves are highly poetic, but Ryman
also moves towards the state of sculpture, with his use of many
different materials, from wood to steel, from fibreglass to
Plexiglas, from cardboard to copper.

It would be hard to see Sol LeWitt's cuboid, mathematical, conceptual sculpture as sensual. LeWitt's angular objects – the frames
of cubes painted white – seem to be the antithesis of sensual art.[12]
His art is all about ideas: the initial idea, the conception, is everything. As LeWitt said:

> *all of the planning and decisions are made beforehand and the execution
> is a perfunctory affair. The idea becomes a machine that makes the art.*[13]

Much of contemporary sculpture consists of hard-edged cubes
or rectangular slabs. Whether this use of such stark mathematical
forms as cubes is rational or intuitive, it takes a scientific,
numerical approach to art to extremes. The idea, Donald Judd
wrote, is to simply do 'the next thing', to do 'one thing after
another'. It is a strategy that is not called a strategy, a systemless
system. Of Frank Stella's paintings, Judd wrote (and this could

apply to Brice Marden's work), that the 'order is not rationalistic and underlying, but is simply order, like that of continuity, one thing after another.'[15]

The notions of Minimalism – seriality, succession, progression, repetition and permutation – have been around for a long time. Leonardo da Vinci, you might say, painted the same picture in different ways, often abandoning projects before completion, while J.M.W. Turner seemed to be painting the same sky, attacking it from thousands of different viewpoints and different locations, from every coastline and lakeside of Britain, to France, Switzerland, Italy and Germany.

But, whether the 'system' is serial or modular, whether there is progression or simply repetition, the notion of Donald Judd's, 'doing the next thing', 'one thing after another', explains so much of Minimal art. It explains so much of Judd's work, for instance, those boxy 'ladders' or stacks of forms ascending to the ceiling in bronze or plastic, and those long lines of crenellations set on a wall. It also describes how artists simply go on making work, as variations, or repetitions, or progressions, like Mark Rothko with his many canvases that explore different combinations of purple or yellow clouds floating on oceans of red or blue, or Ad Reinhardt's seemingly repetitious but actually methodical explorations of five-foot square black canvases. Minimal ethics can produce some extremes of mathematics and seriality.

For British art critic Peter Fuller, Brice Marden and other Minimal artists did not produce a positive æsthetic emptiness, but one which was spiritually bankrupt. Referring to Rudolf Otto's influential book **The Idea of the Holy**, Fuller wrote:

It seems to me that there is every difference in the world between this spiritually replete emptiness and the numbing vacuity of works by artists such as Carl Andre, Agnes Martin, Ellsworth Kelly or Brice Marden.[15]

CHAPTER 5

The Abstract Annunciation: Brice Marden's *Annunciation Series*

SOME THINGS are guaranteed to grab an art critic's attention. Combining modern abstraction with Renaissance themes and iconography is one surefire way, just as incorporating references to William Shakespeare in a contemporary play gives the theatre critic something to chew on. Brice Marden's **Annunciation Series** (1978) has the clearly advertized theme of the Renaissance Annunciation. (Marden said of the **Annunciation Series** that 'I like the idea of subject matter in painting... But, in the end, I just want it to look like a good painting, without any of these things being attached to it' (in J. Lebensztejn).)

   The Annunciation expresses an important doctrinal point in mediæval and Renaissance Christian theology. It stresses the Virgin's total lack of sexual relations, Her purity and perfection,

views which Catholics still endorse (G. Ashe, 63). The Angel
Gabriel greets Mary with the words **Ave Maria, Gratia Plena** – 'hail
Mary, full of grace'. She answers **Ecce ancilla domina** – 'Behold,
the handmaid of the Lord' (J. Metford, 13). In Renaissance
paintings, the Virgin Mary is usually found reading (**Isaiah**, 7:14).
The Archangel often carries a lily, or lilies are seen in the picture –
a symbol of the Virgin's purity. Light streams in through a
window, traditionally symbolizing virginity, but also mythically
representing the Divine Word of God (the root meaning of the
word 'deus' means 'the shining one'). The angel Gabriel tells
Mary She is to bring forth the Son of God. She replies: 'How can
this be, seeing I know not a man?' (**Gospel of St Luke**). As soon as
Mary accepts, She conceives Christ in Her womb. It is verily the
moment when the Word becomes Flesh.

The passage in **The Bible** runs thus:

> Now in the sixth month, the archangel Gabriel was sent from God to a
> city of Galilee, named Nazareth, to a virgin pledged to be married to a
> man whose name was Joseph, of the house of David. The virgin's name
> was Mary. Having come in, the angel said to her, "Rejoice, you highly
> favored one! The Lord is with you. Blessed are you among women!" But
> when she saw him, she was greatly troubled at the saying, and
> considered what kind of salutation this might be. The angel said to her,
> "Don't be afraid, Mary, for you have found favor with God. Behold, you
> will conceive in your womb, and bring forth a son, and will call his name
> 'Jesus.' He will be great, and will be called the Son of the Most High. The
> Lord God will give him the throne of his father, David, and he will reign
> over the house of Jacob forever. There will be no end to his Kingdom."
> Mary said to the angel, "How can this be, seeing I am a virgin?" The
> angel answered her, "The Holy Spirit will come on you, and the power of
> the Most High will overshadow you. Therefore also the holy one who is
> born from you will be called the Son of God. Behold, Elizabeth, your
> relative, also has conceived a son in her old age; and this is the sixth
> month with her who was called barren. For everything spoken by God is
> possible." Mary said, "Behold, the handmaid of the Lord; be it to me
> according to your word." The angel departed from her.

There are (usually five) different types of Annunciation images, depicting different moments in the apostles' story. The most challenging task for the painter is to depict the complex web of emotions in the Annunciation: the simultaneous fear and wonder, doubt and passion of the Virgin Mary. The splendour of the Archangel Gabriel is relatively easy to describe: peacock's feathers do well for his costume and wings. For the Madonna, something more is required, something delicate and poignant. For Mary is required to express joy on one hand, but, as in all Christian religion, there must be humility too.

Fra Roberto Caracciolo organized the Annunciation into fifteen stages in 1489, grouped together in fives under three principal mysteries: the Angelic Mission, the Angelic Salutation, and the Angelic Colloquy.[1] It is in the Colloquy where the real drama of the Annunciation occurs, where there is a small amount of dialogue and negotiation. The five stages, which form the titles of Brice Marden's paintings, are:

1. *Conturbatio* (Disquiet)
2. *Cogitatio* (Reflection
3. *Interrogatio* (Inquiry)
4. *Humiliatio* (Submission)
5. *Meritatio* (Merit)

Most Renaissance **Annunciations** are of the Disquiet or Submission type. The versions of Sandro Botticelli, Fra Filippo Lippi, Leonardo da Vinci and Fra Angelico are clearly of the submissive kind, where the Virgin Mary psychologically prostrates Herself before the Lord, stating that She is His servant. Fra Roberto describes this moment of ritual humiliation thus:

Lowering her head she spoke: Behold the handmaid of the Lord. *She did*

*not say 'Lady'; she did not say 'Queen'. Oh profound humility! oh
extraordinary gentleness! 'Behold,' she said, 'the slave and servant of my
Lord.'*[2]

For feminists, the Annunciation is another example of the Virgin
Mary's passivity. She seems too passive, too humble, too
acquiescent in Her fate. In the Annunciation, Mary is taken by
force, without being able to refuse. Brice Marden's **Annunciation
Series** does not question the patriarchal, traditional nature of the
Annunciation. For him, it is a quiet, mystical moment. Marden's
version of the Annunciation has little to do with 1970s radical
feminism. His **Annunciation Series** has more to do with the
poetry of the event, the tranquil but insistent spirituality of the
Annunciation (the paintings were about 'taking light through',
Marden said in 1989 [PD, 28]).

The German poet Rainer Maria Rilke (1875-926) wrote a
sequence of Madonna poems, his **Marien leben**, or **The Life of the
Virgin Mary**, which expressed some of the sense of quietude and
poetry that Brice Marden's paintings aim for.

> *Nun soll ein neues sein,*
> *von dem der Erdkreis ringender sich weitet.*
> *Wast ist ein Dörnicht uns: Gott fühlt sich ein*
> *in einer Jungfrau Schooss. Ich bin der Schein*
> *von ihrer Innigkeit, der euch geleitet.*

> *[Now shall a new thing be, by which the world shall spread in inter*
> *circles. What is a thornbush to us: God feels his way into a virgin's*
> *womb. I am the shine of her lovingness, that goes with you.]*[3]

Brice Marden's **Annunciation** paintings are each 84 by 96
inches, each constructed out of four panels in oil and wax on
canvas. The vertical canvas panels refer to humanity and the
figure.[4] The vertical panels themselves offer a physical modulation

of the themes and iconography of the **Annunciation Series**. There are two small, 16-inch panels panels in each painting and two larger, 32-inch panels. At the start of the series, in **Conturbatio**, the two thin panels are side by side, on the left of the painting. In the second painting, the narrow panels are separated from each other by the wider panels. In the central painting, **Interrogatio**, the two 16-inch panels are set side by side again, but in the centre, not at the edge of the painting. The fourth image is a reflection of the second painting, panel-wise, and in the fifth picture, **Meritatio**, the panels are at the right-hand side. There is a strong sense of narrative and narrative drive in these paintings, moving inexorably from left to right, from a beginning to an end. Combined with Marden's colors, the panel construction of the paintings offers an abstract equivalent (and commentary upon) the theme of the (Renaissance and Biblical) Annunciation.

The left-to-right movement is a part of Renaissance **Annunciations**. In nearly every **Annunciation** painting of the era the Virgin stands or sits on the right of the picture; the Archangel appears on the left. The spiritual energy flows from left to right, from the angel towards the woman. In some pictures the angel kneels, or leans forward on one foot, stepping forward as if he's just walked into the frame. In some **Annunciations**, Gabriel has an immense kinetic energy, as if he's only just landed on Earth, hot and excited from his journey from Heaven. In Sandro Botticelli's **Annunciation** (1489-90) in the Uffizi Museum, for example, Gabriel is a mass of folds and billowing clothes, bending athletically onto his knees before the Virgin. She, meanwhile, is equally elaborately portrayed in undulating robes, which fall open to reveal Her red dress. The Virgin's agitation in Botticelli's picture causes Her to swerve away from the Archangel, as in Simone Martini's Uffizi painting of the Annunciation (1333). If Gabriel seems full of energy, the Virgin Mary's pose is just as striking: Her whole body twists away the angel, Her knees bent, Her hands lifted in defence before Her.

Color does much of the expressive work in Brice Marden's **Annunciation Series**. Marden uses very bold colors, as in **Thira**. The colors of the **Annunciation Paintings** are distinctly brighter and brasher than those in the monochrome works of the 1960s and early 1970s. Marden employs the primary colors, a predominance of red and green, with the blues softer darker and more restrained, and near blacks and near whites. As with **Thira** and the **Moon** paintings, it is the way Marden sets one color next to another that is really important. Sometimes the comparisons between one color and the next one along can seem startling, as in the unexpected transmission from the light green in **Meritatio** to the bright cream next to it.

Emphasizing the element in the Annunciation of **dialogue**, light panels are set beside dark panels, and red panels next to green. Always there is one then the other, the rhythm of the dialogue is evoked at every moment in the narrative of the five stages of Marden's **Annunciation Series**. The very first contrast in the series, for instance, is between a dark green and a brilliant yellow.

If we read Brice Marden's **Annunciation Series** a little too literally, we can associate the rush of red in the second and third paintings to the Virgin Mary's emotional state. After all, Marden has suggested we read these paintings in terms of emotion and Renaissance iconography. It is significant, then, that, after the dark-yellow-dark green of the first painting, a deep scarlet should appear which is modulated in the second and third paintings. If we keep in mind the dialogue that occurs throughout the Annunciation between the Archangel Gabriel and the Virgin Mary, we can see how one panel relates to what the Angel says, followed by the Madonna's response. For example, in **Cogitatio** , the second painting, there are two colors, red and green. The narrow panel has dark red, which is followed by the broader panel of lighter red. Then there's dark olive green, followed by a mid-green. One color is thus immediately modulated by the next one, one lightens the next. The title, **Cogitatio** (**Reflection**), suggests a stream of thought, so that one thought modulates the preceding one, which is what Marden depicts with his dark then lighter reds and greens.

In the central panel, **Interrogatio** , the dialogue reaches its height, as question and response is fired back and forth between the Archangel and the Madonna. A bright (but deeper) yellow is intercut with a dark vermilion. The colors leap from yellow to red. The dialogue between angel and woman is at its fiercest here, though it is always played out silently, as in all Renaissance **Annunciations**. Not a word is spoken aloud: the Archangel voices his thoughts internally. Ribbons of words fly from the angel to the Madonna in Renaissance **Annunciations** (in Simone Martini's eloquent Uffizi painting). Marden preserves this silent aspect of Renaissance Annunciations. His **Annunciation Series** is, like most of his art, experienced in silence and reflection.

In **Humiliatio**, as one would expect, the colors are at their most muted. Even here, though, there is still a sense of dialogue, of call and response. The painting starts with a near white, in a sense the most 'neutral' (or non-expressive) color in the **Annunciation**

Series. Then follows three dark colors, a near-black, a dark ultramarine and a dark viridian. **Humiliatio** is the moment when the Virgin Mary bows down low before the Archangel Gabriel and the Lord. The angel's work is all over, it seems. He has fulfilled his mission, conveyed his message, impregnated the Virgin. It is not over for the Madonna yet, however. From Her position as 'an obscure Jewish wife' (Geoffrey Ashe's phrase), She is catapulted into Christian superstardom, becoming not only the Mother of God but also the Queen of Heaven.

Thus, the last painting, **Meritatio**, offers some form of spiritual triumph for the Virgin Mary. The colors of **Meritatio** are vigorously orchestrated, as in Brice Marden's earlier **Red, Yellow, Blue** paintings. There is no passional crimson here, as in the first three paintings, but that corn yellow does reappear. The shadowy green of the fourth painting, **Humiliatio**, is transformed in the fifth painting into an optimistic emerald. Then comes that wide band of cream, a color which offers a harmony between the clashes of red and yellow of the third panel, **Interrogatio.** The cream color provides a balance of the spiritual forces of the Annunciation. It offers a point of resolution, which is not total, as it cannot be in the Annunciation, for there is still so much of the Christian story to be lived yet. The final two panels of Marden's **Annunciation Series** display again the dualistic nature not only of the Annunciation theme, but of the spiritual quest of Christianity: joy but also pain, salvation but also difficulty, confusion, ambiguity, transcendence but also mortality (symbolized here by a dark and light color, a dark green and a bright yellow).

Brice Marden's **Annunciation Series** draws heavily on Renaissance painting, and offers a commentary upon it. The levels of discourse in the **Annunciation Series** – mid-late 1970s painting, mediæval and Renaissance theology, traditional symbolism, Renaissance painting, other contemporary abstract religious series (Barnett Newman's *Stations of the Cross*, for example) – lean as much towards the Italian Renaissance as to the contemporary American era. Of course, Marden's **Annunciation Series** is a wholly late 20th century product. Yet we can see in it the echoes of, for instance, Fra Angelico. Marden's **Humiliatio** for example, replays and reworks the intense humility and repose found in Fra Angelico's many **Annunciations**. Marden replaces the blue and gold visual poems of Angelico's art with a sombre meditation of humility and acceptance decked out in grave white, black, ultramarine and viridian colors. The **Humiliatio** panels have the **gravitas** and solemnity of Angelico's **Annunciations**. Marden's **Humiliatio** stresses, like Angelico's frescoes in San Marco, Florence, the seriousness of the Virgin Mary accepting the angelic salutation.

The spatial organization of horizontals and verticals in Fra Filippo Lippi's **Annunciation** (1443-50) in Munich can be seen in Brice Marden's **Annunciation Series**. Like Lippi's painting, Marden's canvases explore the complex relationship between spirituality and space, how space is governed by spiritual energies. In the **Interrogatio** panels we can see the architectonics and verticality of Piero della Francesca's **Annunciation** (1455, in Arezzo), in which the Madonna stands rigid and proud like the monumental, Corinthian column beside her. The upright rigidity of the Virgin appears in Piero's other Madonna paintings (the **Madonna della Misericordia**, 1445, and the **Madonna del Parto,** 1450s). The two small 16-inch panels in the centre of Marden's

Interrogatio recall the configuration of Piero's columnar, Annunciate Virgin, as well as Marden's developing interest in Greek architecture, which was to flower with **Thira** and the series of prints of the late 1970s and early 1980s.

The dynamism of Sandro Botticelli's Guardi **Annunciation**, the violence of movement of which unsettled Leonardo da Vinci, is powerfully reformed by Brice Marden in the first stage of the Annunciation, **Conturbatio**. Marden places the two poles of religious/ symbolic color, black and red, at opposite ends of his painting. The narrative movement is unrelenting: the painting moves vigorously from black to red. There is no let-up in the movement, even as the pulses of question and answer modulate the journey. The painting begins with black then yellow, in the two narrow panels, which is like the flash of the Creation, a light shining out of nowhere. From the suddenness of the black and yellow there is the slowness of the green, as if the narrative is the fleet-footed motion of the Archangel encountering some resist-ance on the ground. He does meet with resistance, or a new and powerful player in the Christian Passion story: the Virgin Mary. That opening flash, from black to yellow, dark to light, is slowed up considerably by the expanse of olive green.

But the journey into Christ's life itself is inexorable, and **Conturbatio** ends with a wide expanse of red, the most forceful and lively of all colors. The sheer amount of red in the next two paintings proclaims the **Annunciation Series** to be an important departure for Brice Marden's art. True, he did use crimson in the **Moon** paintings, and in works such as **For Hera**. The combination of the color with the thematic and iconological aspects of the **Annunciation** paintings give it a deeper and more serious meaning than in Marden's previous work. Here the color red must be associated with the central mysteries of Christianity and the Passion. In Marden's paintings, the color red looks forward to the central act of Christianity, the Crucifixion, just as in Renaissance paintings of the Annunciation a little cross, a tree or the passage the Virgin's reading in a book looks forward to the Passion.

Piero della Francesca is an obvious ancestor of Brice Marden's religious paintings, for Piero is one of the most 'abstract' of Renaissance painters, with his explorations of space and perspective. It is a commonplace of art criticism to point out the relationship between Piero's panels of light and Cubism. As important for Marden's art, though, is pre-Renaissance painting. For example, Roman painting, which he looked at for its use of space. Or Byzantine icon paintings, which position figures floating on gold grounds. In Trecento and Quattrocentro Italian painting, we see large, monumental Madonnas set against rich gold. The figures are flat, like Minimal paintings, while the gold ground has no 'space' at all: it suggests the infinity of Heaven, and of divine power. It is in these post-Byzantine icons and altarpieces, then, that we might look for correspondences with Marden's **Annunciation Paintings**, as much as with the more familiar names of Sandro Botticelli, Leonardo da Vinci, Piero della Francesca and Fra Angelico.

Certainly Brice Marden's **Annunciation Series** paintings are among the most successful of contemporary religious paintings. They have the intensity of Emil Nolde's Christologic works, but of course recall some of the great Northern European painters – Jan van Eyck, Rogier van der Weyden and Albrecht Dürer. Marden has successfully combined Christian subjects and motifs with

Renaissance structures and iconography, in a distinctly late 20th
century framework of his own devising. These are Postminimal
paintings which go far beyond the confines of Minimalism. They
open themselves to emotion in ways which some of the more
austere Minimal artists would find disagreeable.

The **Annunciation Series** is definitely religious (disregarding the
artist's own religious beliefs). They tell a sacred story, a myth of a
divine power manifesting itself on Earth, in a womb. Although the
contemporary, postmodern era is thoroughly secular, Marden's
Annunciation Series is founded on an intuition of the sacred.
What Marden has done is to take Renaissance religious iconography and turn it into late 20th century abstract art. In doing so
he activates a web of æsthetic and religious problems surrounding
the representation of the divine.[5] Somehow, the painter has to
make visible what is essentially invisible and intangible: the
sacred, a feeling for the divine. In the Christian tradition, the
figure is predominant. Yet there is a deeply problematic relation
between figuration and the energies of divine power. The solution
of Islamic art, for example, which Ad Reinhardt had sympathy
with, sweeps away figuration and representation, and goes for
abstraction. Marden's **Annunciation Paintings** do not concern
themselves with the historical or sociological or even theological
dimensions of the Annunciation event, but with the spiritual
feelings of it. The Annunciation itself is an impossible moment to
depict. You can show the two figures, the Archangel and the
Madonna, but what is really going on occurs internally – not
simply in the Virgin's womb as She conceives Christ, but in Her
soul, Her heart, Her mind. Marden's solution to the problem of
depiction is a vigorous Post-Painterly Abstraction, founded on

polychromatic transplendency. While Renaissance painters such as Fra Filippo Lippi, Sandro Botticelli, Fra Angelico, Piero della Francesca and Jan van Eyck concentrated on painting the magnificence of the angel, with his huge peacock wings and ornate robe, and the beauty of the Virgin Mary in Her chaste adolescence, Marden is not so specific: his Annunciation occurs in an ambivalent, non-historical, non-geographically-bound space. There are no references to Adam and Eve, no detailed depictions of the Virgin's garden or Her bedroom, no miniature reliefs showing scenes from the **Old Testament**, no columns and arcades, no tiled floors, no distant views of the landscape, no dove flying down from God's hand and no lilies. Yet Marden's **Annunciation Series** is no less 'holy' than Renaissance paintings of the Annunciation.

The Renaissance painters (Piero della Francesca, Fra Angelico, Sandro Botticelli, Fra Filippo Lippi, Rogier van der Weyden) were trying to convey a particular spiritual feeling, comprising notions of humility, purity, divinity, piety and transcendence. Brice Marden showed that he was no less successful in conveying this complex of feelings in his **Annunciation Series** paintings. True, Marden's set of paintings were not commissioned by a church, monastery or ecclesiastical body, were not conceived within the same socio-religious framework, were not intended to be displayed in a religious setting, but this does not invalidate the spiritual authority of the canvases.

CHAPTER **6**

Multi-panel and Monochrome:
The Paintings of the
1960s and 1970s

IN TERMS of color, Brice Marden's paintings of the 1960s and 1970s are sombre, restrained, impenetrable, physical, tactile, and sonorous. When he uses one color, Marden generally fills the whole painting with it; it's an evenly-spread field of color. When he uses two colors, Marden establishes the relationship between them very carefully. In the multi-part paintings, the colors and the panels exist on the same plane, which is smooth and flat (C. Robins, 1984, 182). Marden modulates his colors so that they seem to inhabit the same tone zone, even though they can seem to be from different color families. Although each panel contains different colors, the color value is often the same (G, 19-20).

A painting such as **Three Deliberate Greys for Jasper Johns** (1970, Ottawa, and spelt 'grey' not 'gray') is a work that takes much of its power from the relativity of grey tones. In this homage to (and wry look at) Jasper Johns, Brice Marden explores the interaction of the tonal value of the ubiquitous 1960s 'neutral' color. It is a tribute to Marden's talent that he could make the painting work. After all, the project of making a painting using only grey, without any figurative or representational elements, entirely in abstraction, could have backfired easily. It is the sort of brief, if given to art students, would have them groaning, dissolving into bouts of apathy and dead-ends. Yet Marden's **Three Deliberate Greys for Jasper Johns** is one of his most successful works, the culmination of his exploration of neutral color.

From the beginning, Brice Marden acknowledged the emotional power of color. Underneath the monochrome greys and beiges there is an emotional subtext. Marden associated his 1960s grey color, for example, with depression. He was depressed at the time he made some of the 1960s paintings. A later pen-and-ink set of drawings was entitled **Suicide Notes** (a series of rectangles, some shadowy, some incomplete, some constructed from webs of lines). Marden wanted the viewer to come away from his paintings changed: to go in expecting something, but to get something else. Marden's Post-Painterly Abstract monochrome paintings hide something underneath, which Marden expressed in terms of color:

> *Gray was the way I could deal with color at the time. What I liked about it was how you could twist it, how you could make it be gray, and also be red – how you could get two readings out of one thing.* (AA)

Grey is the supreme color of ambiguity – indeed, it is not even regarded as a color. Grey is not black, nor white, but Brice Marden showed how it could be hot, cold, light, dark, luminous or mat. Using grey gave Marden a severely reduced formalism, which he worked through intensely. The early and mid-1960s monochrome paintings are 'uncompromising', in the sense that they do not leap out at the viewer and lay themselves bare. They are not explicit, not obvious, not immediate, like Jackson Pollock's paintings were. In works such as **Untitled** (1964), **Dylan Study I** (1963, Lausanne), **Decorative Painting** (1964-5, New York), and **Nico's Painting** (1966, Saatchi Collection), Marden explored the Minimal notions of monochrome, seriality, repetition and restraint. The paintings which have one color – **4:1 (for David Novros), Nico's Painting, T.K.B., For Otis, For Me** – are Marden's most 'difficult' works, there is little to be going on with in these paintings, it seems, little to grasp. They are not obviously 'about' anything, they do not have a distinct theme or narrative. There is nothing in them to immediately recognize and discuss. They are not artworks (it's the same with other Minimal works) which translate easily into other media. Marden's paintings exist in themselves, by and for themselves. They seem to be 'spaceless' and 'subjectless', much as Ad Reinhardt called for a 'formless', 'relationless', 'valueless' art of 'nothingness'. Yet Marden's 1960s monochrome paintings do in fact have subjects, forms, themes, narratives.

Most of the mid-1960s monochromes were grey single panels, horizontal format, with a dripped bottom edge. **Wax I** (Brice Marden's first wax painting, 1966, Des Moines), is a dark grey panel, evenly painted, with all sense of allusion, metaphor and emotion seemingly eradicated from it. **Wax I** became the model for many of Marden's subsequent monochrome works. **T.K.B.** (1966, Philip Schrager, Omaha) was a dark grey, sombre painting, as befits a work intended to be an elegy for one of Marden's friends who had overdosed. Two paintings of the same size (69" by 45"), the proportion used for the **Back Series**, were even darker and more sombre than **T.K.B.** Both **For Otis** (1967-69, Zurich) and **For Me** (1967-8, collection: Robert Rauschenberg) were uncompromising vertical panels of an evenly-spread near-black. The sense of mourning is very apparent: the title **For Me** suggests that some of Marden's sense of injustice or suffering was directed at himself.

Throughout his career Brice Marden has made personal statements in his paintings, which refer to particular events from his life. **For Me** is one of those not infrequent autobiographical works, while the **Back Paintings** were about his estrangement from his wife Helen (Marden divorced from his first wife, Pauline, in the mid-1960s, and went to live alone at 76 Jefferson Street, near Chinatown). **Nebraska** (1966) was a smaller single panel (58 by 72 inches), in a mid-grey which referred, in the Alfred Stieglitz-equivalent fashion, to landscape. (Marden had made sketches of rectangular images while driving through Nebraska).

A series of drawings of the mid-1960s period (done in charcoal; charcoal and graphite; graphite and beeswax; and oil and wax crayon), were called **Untitled** and featured dense black rectangles. Brice Marden's drawings of this time were every bit as uncompromising in their pursuit of formal perfection. Sometimes the drawings were made in graphite and silkscreen on paper, but the effect was the same: very dense black rectangles. Only in a few drawings was a grid perceptible underneath the layers of black graphite, as in **Patent Leather Valentine** (1967, Helen Harrington Marden) and **Untitled** (1968, Mrs V.W. Ganz). Some of these mid-1960s drawings emulated the paintings with their lower edge left bare to catch the drips. Marden simulated paint drips by leaving a gap then going partially over it: in, for instance, **Teddy's Drawing** (1965, collection: E.R. Hudson) and **Untitled** (1966, collection: Roy Lichenstein).

What was Brice Marden trying to do with his color? In statements and interviews, we can piece together some of his aims. In Marden's art, color becomes identified with physical space, with the physicality of the canvas and its support. Like many painters throughout history, Marden regarded color as a physical thing, something that not only affected the eyes, but could be felt, smelt, tasted, heard. Everyone knows how 'loud' red can be (a color Marden studiously avoided in most of his 1960s paintings). Marden spoke of color in 1971 in terms of 'character' and 'weight':

Color as character
Color as weight
Color as color
Color as color value (W, 56)

Marden spoke of the relationship between color and space, how colors relate to the outside edges of a painting, how colors create and modulate the formal (= spiritual) tensions of a painting.

A color should turn back into itself.
It should reveal itself to you while, at the same time, it evades you. (W, 56)

Here Brice Marden expresses one of his fundamental precepts: that the artwork should simultaneously pull the viewer in, and evade them. Color is meant to entice, as well as be ambiguous. Marden's paintings are meant to invite absorption, as well as distantiation. The paintings are sensual, mesmeric objects, inviting intimacy, and cool, detached objects, commanding distance. The ambivalence of the paintings perhaps suggests why people are sometimes not sure how to respond to them. With Marden's art however, as we have seen, if one sticks to the precepts of High Modernism, of the beauty of the art object, one cannot go far wrong. If one trusts one's senses, that is, one can respond wholly to the paintings.

So tightly valued, in terms of color, were Brice Marden's 1960s monochrome paintings, it was startling to move from the single color to the multiple color paintings. One got used to staring at a single color, such as the greyish blue of **4:1 (For David Novros**) or **Nico's Painting,** so that a painting with two colors, such as **Blunder** (1969, Saatchi), seemed a dramatic departure. This shows how powerful Marden's monochrome paintings were/ are: they could hypnotize with their large areas of grey or ochre. They were subtle but insistent mesmeric artworks, pulling the spectator in with sensual promises. More than almost any other painter of the 20th century, Brice Marden evoked a pre-œdipal maternal world, a womb-realm which recalls Julia Kristeva's **chora** and semiotic modality. Anxiety, ambiguity, confusion, loss and aggression were dissolved in Marden's amniotic panels of pale blue, grey and mahogany.

Brice Marden's 1960s palette kept to the grey and blue end of the scale. Underneath there were hints (tints) of warmer colors, but these were always carefully restrained, and modulated by extensive reaches of grey and blue. Paintings such as **The Dylan Karina Painting** (1969, Saatchi) were founded on a light ochre: in two panels, the beige on the left is slightly, only slightly, darker than the beige in the right panel. **Grand Street** (1969) steps away from the predominance of grey or blue into using purple – but this light lilac is restrained on either side by same-sized panels of grey and pale turquoise. **Point to Point,** from the same year (1969), is an inexplicable expanse of mid-brown, over two and a half metres of it. **Parks (for Van Dyke Parks)** (1968-9, Minnea-polis) is another beige painting, a triptych of narrow vertical panels, with the artist cleverly harmonizing the cooler left panel with the warmer hues of the right panel – the centre panel unites the two with a passive, solid grey-ochre. **Point** (1969, New York) is a triptych (53 by 106.3 inches) of pale blues, as inexplicable as **Point to Point**, yet as hypnotic. **Point** looks directly towards the **Grove Group** of the early 1970s, with its exploration of interconnected blue hues.

The more poetically titled **D'après la Marquise de la Solana** (also 1969, Guggenheim), is one of the lusher multi-panel works of the late 1960s: moving from one of Brice Marden's 'implac-able' mid-greys in the left-hand panel to a similarly-toned grey with a sheen of lilac shone over it in the centre panel; finally, a light pink resides in the right-hand panel, the kind of shell pink Mark Rothko employed in his late oil on paper sketches. In **Range** (1970, Princeton), Marden places a rich yellow onto the left-hand panel of a triptych – but the other two panels, as with **D'après la Marquise de la Solana**, are kept in the mid-grey mid-tone zone. **Fave** (1968-9, University of Texas), goes back to the very light tones of the early works (such as **Pair** and **Return I**). Two similarly-toned colors stand beside each other in two vertical panels, a format that recalls **For Helen** and **Pair.** The colors are pulled right back, so that the yellow on the left is extremely pale – more cream than yellow, more white than cream. It is one of those 'off whites' that household paint manufacturers invent new names for (light buttercup yellow, Moroccan melon, etc).

Clearly the realm Brice Marden was aiming for was quite from different from that of Roy Lichenstein, say, or Judy Pfaff. Of course, it might seem wholly inappropriate to compare Marden's 1960s project with that of Lichenstein or Pfaff, for he is so different. But then, Marden is different even from those artists most closely associated with him – Robert Ryman, Agnes Martin, Robert Mangold, Donald Judd and Jules Olitski. Marden is in a world of his own. One can make cultural comparisons, but this is only partially helpful. One only has to compare the subdued grey and pale cobalt panels of Brice Marden with the incredibly vivacious, multicolor of Frank Stella's **Protractor** series of the Sixties to see how far Marden was from mainstream Minimalism, Colorfield and Hard Edge Painting and most Post-Painterly Abstraction.

For some, Brice Marden's abstract paintings created a response of 'so what?' His paintings were beautiful and sensual (a 'beautiful presence and another and another and another', as one critic put it), but to what end? (C. Robins, 1976, 19). But beyond the difficulty and restraint of Marden's paintings, there was quite a bit going on. It's the same with other Minimalist and Post-Painterly and Process/ Serial art. The closer one looks, the busier and more complex and sensual these works become. A cursory glance at Robert Ryman's paintings, for example, would see nothing but white squares of different sizes (typically 60 or 72 inches square). Looking closer, however, one saw that Ryman was meticulously and vigorously exploring the relationships between color and support, between shape and color, between objectification and illusion, and between abstraction and figuration. Far from being all the same monotonous white-on-white, Ryman's paintings were all individual. Each one had its own specifications of frame size and support (aluminium, canvas, plastic, wood, fibreglass). There were clips around the edge of some paintings, while others were bolted to the wall.

Another white-on-white Minimal painter, Agnes Martin, also seemed to have little of interest happening in her paintings. When you looked closer, you saw different grids, different ways of marking the grid (gold leaf, pencil, ink). Sometimes the grid was very tight and compact, with a tiny rectangle being described; sometimes there was a web of horizontal lines, widely spaced; sometimes the white was attenuated by a faint pink or grey or cream between each set of horizontal bands. Then take Donald Judd. His works seem to be firmly fixed in a monotonous rectangular view of the world. It seemed to be an arid, vacuous world of boxes and more boxes. Looking closer, one saw that there was a great sense of play and humour at work in the choice of materials (sometimes wood, sometimes steel, or glass, or copper, or lacquer, or Plexiglas). Sometimes Judd's serial boxes were open, and one could see inside them; at other times, Judd placed colored Plexiglas over the end, and the interior was hidden or vaguely discernible; sometimes the boxes were sprayed with Harley Davidson motorbike lacquer and enamel, so they'd be bright green, or red. Seemingly hollow and fragile, with their thin walls, Judd's boxes were also constructed from strong materials, and were fixed, immobile, to the wall. There was in fact a lot going in Judd's works.

What appeared from a distance in Minimalism to be a uniform set of paintings or sculptures turned out to be a collection of individual works, each created with its own set of æsthetic considerations. What Marden, Agnes Martin, Robert Ryman, Donald Judd and Sol LeWitt were doing was exploring art with an apparently narrow or 'minimal' set of æsthetic constraints. When you looked closer, the sense of narrowness and limitation disappeared. The feeling of openness and play blossomed.

NEW COLOURS OF THE 1970s
◆

In the early 1970s Brice Marden began to loosen up his palette and introduce much deeper, more saturated colors – and tones. Nature was also more apparent, in series of paintings such as the **Grove Group** and the **Sea Paintings**. The **Sea Paintings** introduced much deeper tones, or rather, much stronger contrasts between one tone and the next. Instead of gentle modulations between one panel and another, Marden was happy to make sudden contrasts and leaps. Thus, in **Red, Yellow, Blue** (1974), the red is very dark, while the yellow, as usual in Marden's art, is light. The result is a sharp leap in tone from the left to the middle panel, which the right hand (blue) panel helps to modulate by its tone, which is mid-way between the red and yellow.

Paintings such as **To Corfu**, **Le Mien** and **Morada**, from the mid-1970s, feature the narrow vertical panels which Brice Marden used so effectively in the **Annunciation Series**. Contemporary prints, such as **Untitled** (1973), also feature vertical columns. New colors in the Marden canon (part of his 'red yellow blue' period) appeared in **Morada** (1976, Stedelijk Museum, Amsterdam) and **Le Mien** (1976, Zurich): a dark, damson red, which's followed, in both paintings, by a mid-grey or greyish-blue. In **Morada** we find the usual colors of Marden's 1970s Greek period: olive greens, light greys, and a dark grey. Into this mélange of familiar light/ mid/ dark greys, the damson hue is really surprising. It is, literally, a 'splash' of color – living color, the color of life (blood, anger, passion, fecundity). Imagine this damson-red entering Marden's austere Greek paintings, such as **Lethykos, Moon I** and any of the **Grove Group Paintings**. In **Le Mien** the damson color takes up one of the wide panels on the left, and is echoed by the mid-red in the right-hand narrow panel. Against these sonorous hues, Marden places his olive grove greens and greys. The painting is symmetrical, in terms of color (though not with the perfect symmetry of **Lethykos (for Tonto)**): warm green is set against deep crimson; lighter red is set against light grey.

In these paintings of the late 1960s and early 1970s, Brice Marden allowed his palette to open up, introducing warm, mid-earth-browns in **For Pearl**, lemon yellows in **Rodeo** and buttercup yellows in **Range, First Figure (Homage to Courbet)** and **Starter**, and one of Marden's most radiant colors, the orangey-red outer panels of **Pumpkin Plumb**. The outer panels in **For Pearl** (1970,

Lannan Foundation, Los Angeles) contain and moderate the warmest color, the earthy brown, with two more restrained hues (a grey-blue on the left, and a sand tint on the right). **Rodeo** (1971, Lannan Foundation) is one of the first of Marden's horizontal format dual color paintings: an expanse of lemon yellow in the upper half; dark slate grey in the lower half.

Untitled (1971-2, Walker Art Center, Minneapolis) is unusual for Brice Marden at this period: three warm colors, rather than, as is more usual, one warm and two cooler colors. The central band of light orange is modulated and contained by the outer panels of light carmine. The colors in **For Pearl** and **Untitled** are unusual in Marden's art of this time. In **First Figure (Homage to Courbet)**, the usual three Marden panels are set on top of each other, unusually, creating a tower of three near-square panels. The colors, crowned with a mustard yellow in the upper panel, are those of 1970s works such as **Summer Table, Range** and **Starter** (yellow plus a light and dark neutral color). **Pumpkin Plumb** (1970/ 73, collect- ion: Helen Harrington Marden), contains a vivid contrast between the subdued grey of the 1960s monochrome paintings (in the central panel) and the bright orange, a hue which looked towards the primary colors of the **Red, Yellow, Blue** series of the following year (1974). **Summer Table** (1972-3, Whitney, New York) uses the color-configuration of **Range, First Figure (Homage to Courbet)** and **Starter** : a warm yellow panel in amongst two cooler panels. **Summer Table** is clearly a part of the (Greek) landscape works of the first half of the 1970s (the **Grove Group** and **Sea Paintings**). The warm color is at the centre, but the flanking two blues (one pale, one dark) cannot restrain it. The yellow of **Summer Table** is dominant, overwhelming the outer panels. The structure of the three rectangular panels in a horiz-ontal format of **Summer Table** recalls **Point, Range** and the **Moon Series**. The sullen, recalcitrant greys and blues of the 1960s monochromes are left behind decisively with paintings such as **Summer Table, Pumpkin Plumb** and the **Red, Yellow, Blue Series**. With his new, colorful palette, Marden's art gained a new intensity, no longer tied to an introspective, 'depressed' mood.

Miranda (1972, New York) is three panels of closely-valued color in a horizontal format making a 72 by 72 inch square. The allusions to landscape in the upper olive-grey-green, middle mid-blue and lower sand-earth colors are unmistakable. **Blue Painting** (1972, private collection) is also a part of the group of landscape-based works of the early 1970s. **Blue Painting**, like the **Moon, Hera,** and **Red, Yellow, Blue** paintings, is a vertical three-panel configuration. The colors are those of the **Grove Group** and **Sea Paintings** (light and mid-toned blues). In **Blue Painting** Marden explores the sense of narrative and progression (moving from light through mid to dark blue), which became increasingly important (culminating in the **Annunciation Series**).

Two paintings based on Brice Marden's experience in Morocco also employed earthy colors, like **Starter** and **Summer Table**. Both **Moroccan Painting** (1978, New York) and **Helen's Moroccan Painting** (1979, collection: Helen Harrington Marden) set a mid-green against an earth red-brown. In the former work the panels are side by side vertically, in the latter they are placed one above the other (this vertical format was another reworking of a format used in the early 1970s). In both the effect is of an exploration of landscape; in this case, a response to the particular landscape of Morocco, with its abundant greenery that grows out of what appears to be nothing but dust and desert. Such deep green plants amongst such seemingly arid, barren soil is an astonishment to the traveller used to the lush green of temperate Northern Europe and America's East Coast. Marden's Moroccan panels explore the wonder of the North African landscape, where the dry, apparently lifeless browns of **Hydra** and the early **Untitled** paintings give way to a luscious, fertile green.

Starter (1971, Zurich) contains a warm, buttery yellow (like **Range** and **Untitled**). What is unusual about **Starter**, though, is not the configuration a single color on each of the three panels, in the traditional Mardenesque manner, but the proportion of the painting. It is very wide (3ft high but 8ft across), a proportion that recalls some of the expansive canvases of Abstract Expressionism (Jackson Pollock, Barnett Newman, and Robert Motherwell), and also Kenneth Noland and Morris Louis. Later paintings of Brice Marden's were wider than **Starter** (such as **Moon I** at 120 inches, the **Grove Group** at 108 inches, and **Thira** at an unusual 180 inches), but **Starter** appears so wide and expansive because the panels run across the width of this wide painting.

These hues broaden considerably the narrow range of colors Brice Marden had employed in works such as **For Otis, T.K.B., Wax I, Nebraska** and **Decorative Painting**. In those 1960s mono-chromes, Marden seemed to be working in the rarefied and extreme realm of abstraction occupied by the likes of Ad Reinhardt and Mark Rothko's later work; with the post-1969 multi-panel paintings, and the new, luminous palette, Marden joined the ranks of Post-Painterly Abstract artists, such as the art of Morris Louis, Frank Stella, Kenneth Noland, Richard Diebenkorn and Ellsworth Kelly. Even so, paintings such as **Rodeo, For Pearl,**

D'après la Marquise de la Solana, Point and **Starter** and **Miranda** were still more severe and restrained than anything in the art of Louis, Stella, Noland, Kelly or Diebenkorn.

In amongst the more colorful works of the 1970s (such as **Starter** and the **Red, Yellow, Blue** series), there were still ascetic greys and near-blues, such as in **Gober** (1971, Spiegel Family Collection). This is a narrow vertical dual-color panel whose two muted greys look straight back to the **Untitleds** of the early 1960s. The first **Hydra** (1972, New York), too, is extremely closed-in and muted, quite unlike the later hymns to the Greek landscape (such as **Thira** and the **Grove Group**). **Shunt** (1972, New York) is also restrained, in **Hydra**-like beiges and greys. In amongst the many colorful paintings of the first half of the Seventies, then (such as **Pumpkin Plumb, Blue Painting, Starter, For Hera**), Brice Marden was still producing quiet panels in earth, grey, olive and brown hues (**Hydra, Shunt, Gober, Three Deliberate Greys for Jasper Johns** and so on). Even with a subject such as the iconoclastic rock star Patti Smith, Marden produced a piece in subdued light and dark greys (**Star (For Patti Smith)** , 1972/ 74, private collection).

THE *RED, YELLOW, BLUE SERIES*
◆

The **Red, Yellow, Blue** paintings, all made in 1974, are 74 by 72 inches over three equal vertical panels. They are Brice Marden's brightest works. They show a return to (or acknowledgment of) the primary colors of the 1960s, which played such a prominent part in the art of painters such as Frank Stella, Kenneth Noland and Ellsworth Kelly. Marden's use of the three primary colors, however, is not straightforward, as one might expect. The first **Red, Yellow, Blue** (Albright-Knox Art Gallery, Buffalo) is the most straightforward: the red, yellow and blue are all mid-tones, middle hues. The red is a poster paint red, and the yellow is a melon or lemon yellow, a color found in every child's watercolor paintbox. The blue, too, is an ordinary ultramarine, not the azure of Renaissance Madonnas or the Greek sky or sea. Like a flag, **Red, Yellow, Blue I**, displays its colors without hiding anything, without vacillation.

   Red, Yellow, Blue II (Museum of Contemporary Art, Los Angeles) is quite different. For a start it moves from yellow through blue to red (the third painting goes from blue through red to yellow). The yellow veers towards orange (though not quite as radiant as the orange wings in **Pumpkin Plumb**). The blue recedes dramatically into the background, behind the yellow and red: it is a metallic grey-blue. The red, meanwhile, has also deepened; it looks forward to the earthy, rich reds of the **Thira**-type paintings. In the third **Red, Yellow, Blue** (collection: M. & J. Ovitz, Los Angeles), the blue has darkened to a near-black, while the yellow has lightened, to the earthy, buttercup yellow of **Range, Starter** and **Conturbatio**; the red remains the same.

The progression, from the first **Red, Yellow, Blue** through the series, is towards complexity and ambiguity. What begins as a seemingly simple set of primary colors is soon modulated into earthier, more opaque and complex colors. Although, unusually, Brice Marden names the colors he's employing, he soon veers from the accepted, traditional primary colors. Indeed, he shows that there is perhaps no such thing as an 'objective', agreed primary color: soon he is experimenting with different combinations of colors, so that the blue steadily darkens, and the yellow starts as a lemon yellow, moves through light orange to a subdued yellow.

Although the early 1970s paintings were a lot brighter and richer in color than the monochromes of the 1960s, some people might still find them subdued and sombre as artworks. Despite the luxuriance of the color, the 1970s oil and wax paintings were still very restrained – compared to other works of art of the time (such as Andy Warhol's Pop Art screenprints, or Lynda Benglis's poured polyurethane artworks).

One always has to sink down into Brice Marden's paintings, much as Meister Eckhart spoke of sinking down into nothingness, or the Zen Buddhists speak of sinking down into meditation. Many people are simply not prepared to do that – they haven't got time, they say, they're too busy, there's nothing to grasp onto in these huge abstract panels of reticent oil and wax.

Yet Brice Marden's paintings are very lush, if one can approach them in the right way: even the austere, introspective 1960s monochromes are actually opulent. It is a question of levels. If we speak of Marden's color brightening and opening out in the early 1970s, we might say that his mid-1960s monochromes were also bright and rich – but in their own, careful, moderate way. Besides, Marden did not abandon the ash grey or wan ultramarine of the 1960s: these colors appear in paintings such as **Lethykos (For Tonto)** of 1976, **Moon I** (1977, both in private collections) and **Winter Painting**, as well as the fourth painting of the **Annunciation Series**, **Humiliato**.

WINTER PAINTING **AND** *SEASONS*
◆

In **Winter Painting** (1973-5, Stedelijk Museum) one sees the sense of narrative development which would become such an import-ant part of the **Annunciation Series**. That is, Brice Marden con-ceives of a movement from left to right, from one panel, with its own color and tone, to the next, and so on. **Winter Painting** has an overt theme, as does the series of four interconnected paint-ings, which also constitute a single painting, **Seasons** (1975, Menil Foundation, Houston). No explanation is needed here in these four panels, which do not, unusually, touch at their edges (like the widely-spaced early two-panel works **Pair** and **For Helen**). The colors in **The Seasons** range from a very light green on the left (Spring) through a mid-green (Summer) to the light grey of Autumn and the darkest tone, the greyish-blue of Winter. You don't have to be a poet to interpret these abstract panels: all you need is the title, **Seasons**, and you're away.

   The Seasons is a large work – all together the four vertical panels stretch to 252 inches horizontally. This sort of scale (21 feet) is usually reserved for the monumentality of Abstract Expressionism (again, Barnett Newman and Robert Motherwell), or later Post-Painterly Abstractionists, such as Morris Louis or Frank Stella. In Brice Marden's **Seasons**, the scale seems quite in keeping with the aims of the work, and is integrated to the other formal concerns, such as the relation of the colors to each other. So adept is Marden's control of his colors and tones it doesn't matter that **The Seasons** approaches the 'monumental' scale of Barnett Newman or Robert Motherwell. The colors, for example, are pulled back so carefully, there is only one 'warm' hue, the yellowy-green on the left. **The Seasons** is not an overwhelming, consuming painting, like some of the Abstract Expressionists' massive canvases. Indeed, as with certain works by Newman and Motherwell and Ellsworth Kelly, tranquillity and passivity is more the order of Marden's **Seasons**.

GROVE GROUP
◆

The **Grove Group** paintings are in the landscape or horizontal format, like other paintings that referred to nature (**Seasons, Summer Table, Winter Painting, Moon I, Thira** and **Gulf**). The thematic dimension of the **Grove Group** is that they are about, well, olive groves; or, more specifically, they take as their departure point Brice Marden's experience of sitting in olive groves. The olive dominates so much of Greece. Indeed, Lawrence Durrell speaks of the Mediterranean as that area marked out by the olive tree. The shiny, silvery underside of the leaves, and the dark tops of the leaves, the extraordinary twisted trunks and branches, the sound of leaves in the wind, the shelter they offer from the noonday sun, all these aspects and more of olive trees would interest a poetic painter such as Brice Marden. He is an artist who comes across more and more as someone who has spent a long and careful time observing nature. His paintings are born out of lengthy immersions in the natural world. He wrote in his notebooks of the importance of observing nature, and of feeling a part of nature, even though this absorption in nature can be problematic (Grove, 26-27). Nature is the teacher, the inspiration, the starting-point for many of Marden's works.

The **Grove Group** employ 'natural' colors, the blues, greens and greys one finds in the natural world. The **Grove Group** paintings are large – the five paintings are 72 by 108 inches. The series begins with a single-color panel, one of Brice Marden's largest expanses of a single hue (**Grove Group I**, 1973, MOMA, New York). The sheer scale and breadth of **Grove Group I** invites comparisons with Barnett Newman, but how subdued Marden's painting is compared to the sonorous ultramarines of Barnett Newman's works (**Cathedra** [1951, Amsterdam], for example). The expanse of blue is consuming, especially as, in **Grove Group II**, the soft cobalt on the left is only partially held back by the darker, mid-ultramarine. **Grove Group III** (1973-80, private collection) is in the familiar 1970s Marden horizontal tripartite format (there are two three-panel **Grove Group** paintings, two dual-plane pieces, and one single panel, **Grove Group I**). **Grove**

Group III, which was reworked in 1980, does not contain blue, like **Grove Group I** or **Grove Group V**. Instead, Marden concentrates, as in other Greek/ Hydra paintings, such as **Lethykos,** on his beloved greys. A pale greeny-grey begins the three-panel work, with a very light grey in the centre. Harnessing these pale greys is a dark grey in the right-hand panel, bringing the painting down to Earth.

Grove Group V (1976, Chicago) is a much warmer painting than some of the other **Grove Groups**: a panel (horizontal this time) of a pale sky blue is at the centre of this painting. A simplistic analogy may be the sky (or sea) glimpsed between the green of the olive leaves. In **Grove Group V** Brice Marden reprises the mid-green of **Grove Group I**, which sandwiches the sky blue panel. In the **Grove Group** paintings the paint reaches right to every edge. There is no strip of canvas kept bare, as in the mid-1960s monochromes.

Like subsequent multi-panel paintings of the 1970s, the **Grove Group** paintings are self-contained, they offer a unified sense of space, with none of the relics of gesture that occurred in the single panel paintings of the 1960s with their strip of splashed or runny paint (Brice Marden's paintings, a critic writes, follow the rule that 'a painting contains within itself its **raison d'être**').[1]

Of all Brice Marden's paintings, the **Grove Group** are among his most tranquil and self-absorbed. They have a mute passivity, which one discerns elsewhere – in the **Back Series** or in **Lethykos (For Tonto)** – but the **Grove Group** paintings are not aligned with the emotions of depression and anxiety, which were so much a part of the 1960s monochrome paintings.

THE *MOON PAINTINGS* AND THE GODDESS
◆

The **Moon Paintings** and related works such as **For Hera** (1977, private collection, Zurich) have mythological themes. In the early 1970s Brice Marden began to read up about mythological matters. He read, like many others, Robert Graves, Aleister Crowley, alchemical texts, books on sacred Greek architecture (Vincent Scull's **Earth, The Temple and the Gods**). Marden's interest in alchemy tied in with his love of ancient Greek art and architecture; the print portfolio **12 Views For Caroline Tatyana** , for instance, combined the Greek **thira** or door motif with alchemical considerations of color. Marden regarded his commission for the stained glass at Basle (made around the same time – late 1970s) in alchemical terms: he thought an alchemical transformation might actually be possible if he 'mixed the colors absolutely right' (P, 44). As he made the stained glass he knew he was working with the materials and modes of mediæval alchemists.

Robert Graves' deeply poetic 1946 book **The White Goddess** (and to a lesser extent his **Greek Myths**) proposes a cult of the Goddess or 'Single Poetic Theme', which pivoted around a heterosexual and slavish love of women. The Muse poet served one person, his Muse, who was an incarnation of the ancient Goddess, variously named Isis, Ishtar, Diana, Venus, Hecate, Kali, and so on. The Goddess came down and 'rode' the woman. The Goddess presided over the key realms of life: birth, love and death. Brice Marden had already shown himself to be something of a Muse artist: his **Back Series** was dedicated to and about his wife, Helen Marden, although Marden enshrined her in an ambiguous fashion. (Graves too, like Muse poets before him –

John Skelton, Edmund Spenser, Dante Alighieri, John Donne, Francesco Petrarch, Torquato Tasso – was ambivalent about his beloved).

Robert Graves spoke of three stages of life, and Brice Marden had long employed the symbolism of the number three. Not only are there many three-panelled paintings, the number three (as well as seven) is crucial to **Thira** and related images. Marden spoke of the purity and power of three, of triads and trinities. The tripartite composition of the three three-panelled **Moon Paintings** was carefully worked out; the proportion of the **Moon Paintings** is the same as that used in the **Five Threes** print series. Marden knew something of numerology; he had read alchemical treatises, as well as occultists such as Aleister Crowley, but made it more explicit in the **Moon Paintings**.

Robert Graves spoke of birth, love and death, and gave them each a color, just as the alchemists did. White was linked with birth, childhood and virginity, symbolized in 'female' terms by the virgin and bride. Red was the passion and fullness of life, symbolized by the woman as lover and mother. Black was death and the unknown, symbolized by the hag or witch. The White Goddess was Diana, Athena; the Red Goddess was the Love Goddesses Venus and Isis; Hecate, Kali and Medusa were the Black Goddess.

In alchemy, the stages of questing for the elixir or philosophical stone or gold move from white through red to black. Sometimes a yellow and a purple stage is added – as by the early Greek alchemical texts. Brice Marden's **Moon III** (1977, private collection, Zurich) follows very precisely the Gravesian/ alchemical progression from white through red to black. In Marden's painting, the narrative is clear: from the White Goddess of childhood, purity, youth and virginity; through the Red Goddess of passion, sex, fullness and motherhood; to the Black Goddess of old age and death, the invisible and the unknown. In short, Marden's **Moon III** is a Goddess painting, which one can read, if one likes, as wholly derived from Robert Graves' Triple Goddess and **The White Goddess**.

For Hera, meanwhile, takes one aspect of the Goddess, framing the central, impenetrable black column with two red panels. The symmetry of **For Hera** makes this a meditative, static painting, rather than transitional and narrative, like **Moon III** or the **Annunciation Series**. **For Hera** pulls the spectator towards the centre of the image: many of Brice Marden's other images do this: **Thira**, for example, and the print series divided into three equal parts, such as **Five Plates** and **Five Threes**. The print series associated with the **Moon Paintings** and **For Hera**, **Five Threes** (1976-7), gravitate the eye towards the centre of the image. The fourth and fifth of the prints leap from black to the white to black again, and white to black and white again. Seen in reproductions, these prints look like black-and-white images of flags, which have the same bold simplicity. In **For Hera**, the color red raises the painting into a different world from the stark signification of flags and signals. The combination of a medium red and near-black make this very much a painting about maturity, passion, about being firmly in the midst of life.

Moon I (private collection, Virginia), in contrast with the passionate scarlets and blacks of **For Hera** and **Moon III,** is cool and meditative. **Moon I** is not so much about a Gravesian Goddess cult as about the sense of time and change and cycles surrounding the moon. The colors of **Moon I** are of the night, the liquid, ethereal, mysterious night and the glimpse of a full moon: two midnight blue panels frame a silvery white central panel. At the centre the abstract equivalent of a full moon; at the two sides, the fade into nighttime. Brice Marden shows the transition from dark to light and back again to dark, the rise/ fall, wax/ wane, ascent/ descent of the moon, and of the seasons and nature. The three panels can be seen as abstract equivalents of the three phases of the moon: waxing, full, and waning. Poets have long celebrated the powers of nighttime (such as William Shakespeare, Dante Alighieri, Rainer Maria Rilke and Matsuo Basho), but it is not such a large part of the history of painting. Marden would have been aware of the moon in his travels on foot and by boat around the islands of Greece. If he stared at the sea for the whole of the voyage to Patras, as he said, he would be the sort of person who is aware of the moon. Most magical of celestial objects, the moon dominates open, rocky, sea-skirted landscapes like Greece.

This is Tu Fu's poem 'Full Moon':

Isolate and full, the moon
Floats over the house by the river.
Into the night the cold water rushes away below the gate.
The bright gold spilled on the river is never still.
The brilliance of my quilt is greater than precious silk.
The circle without blemish.
The empty mountains without sound.
The moon hangs in the vacant, wide constellations.
Pine cones drop in the old garden.
The senna trees bloom.
The same clear glory extends for ten thousand miles.

CHAPTER 7

Greece, the Passion and *Thira*

GREECE IS very important for Brice Marden, and its influence permeates his art. In the Greek landscape, the elements which are dominant are the sky and the sea, which appear in not a few of Marden's paintings. Art terrorist Yves Klein had the inspiration for his famous 'International Klein Blue' from looking at the sheltering sky of the Mediterranean. Lawrence Durrell (Brice Marden had read **The Alexandria Quartet**) has written poetically of Greece's stark, lyrical landscape. In **Reflections on a Marine Venus**, one of Durrell's 'island books', he writes:

> *Then Greece: the vertical, masculine, adventurous consciousness of the archipelago, with its mental anarchy and indiscipline touched everywhere with the taste for agnosticism and spare living. Greece born into the sexual intoxication of the light, which seem to shine upwards from inside the very earth, to illuminate these bare acres of squill and*

asphodel.[1]

Lawrence Durrell evokes the 'blue silence' of Greece, the 'dark crystal' of Greece, the electric blue light which bounces around the rocks, in the poem 'Limits: Mykonos Windmills':

> *The pure form, then, must be the blue silence*
> *And the archaic shape of whiteness posed*
> *On blueness utterly bemused, a sort of coyness*
> *Which garners the wind of the four quarters.*
> (*The Mediterranean Shore*, 144)

This is a stanza from 'On Ithaca Standing':

> *Tread softly, for here you stand*
> *On miracle ground, boy.*
> *A breath would cloud this water of glass,*
> *Honey, bush, berry and swallow.*
> *This rock, then, is more pastoral, than*
> *Arcadia is, Illyria was.*
> (*Collected Poems*, 111)

This picture painted in 'The Anecdotes' of Rhodes is another typical Durrellian scene: the languor, the boats, the cicadas, the figs, and Spring:

> *Anonymous hand, record one afternoon,*
> *In May, some time before the fig-leaf:*
> *Boats lying idle in the sky, a town*
> *Thrown as on a screen of watered silk,*
> *Lying on its side, reddish and soluble,*
> *A sheet of glass leading down into the sea...*
> *Down here an idle boy catches a cicada:*
> *Imprisons it, laughing, in his sister's cloak*
> *In whose warm folds the silly creature sings.*
> (*Collected Poems*, 204)

Greece is the country of the 'big blue', the blue on blue, which Brice Marden has written of in his notebooks:

We swam in the sea today as lovers. The sea was blue, so very blue, the blues of the Madonnas, those most precious blues. One looks up and there are the rocks. Hydra rocks, the pines bending to the winds, echoing the bends the rocks have undergone for so many years. Nature. Forces... Remember immersion – water – land – sky – the all.[2]

The sense of a bright and timeless Greek light informs how some of Brice Marden's paintings look. It is a light that recalls Oriental art, the open voids of Chinese landscape painting, the art of ancient Egyptian friezes, Roman painting and Classical Greek sculpture. Marden's abstract landscapes employ an archaic light which looks back to ancient art. It is a light that recalls the sacred, for light itself is one of the primary, if not **the** primary manifestations of the sacred. Mircea Eliade believes that the sky is the first object of transcendence and the sacred:

I believe, personally, that it is through consideration of the sky's immensity that man is led to a revelation of transcendence, of the sacred. (1984, 162)

SEA PAINTINGS
◆

The sheer number of paintings that deal with Greece, or the sea, attest to the significance the Mediterranean country had (and has) for Brice Marden. Hydra, where he has a house, appears in many works: in the early 1970s multi-panel oil and wax paintings, in the 1979 **Hydra Group**, 1987's **Hydra** (Art Institute of Chicago), and again in the **Hydra (Summer 1990) Series** of 'calligraphic' paintings. The **Sea Paintings** were about the sea, as one might expect. Like **To Corfu, Towards Brindisi,** the three **Hydra** paintings and **Adriatic,** the **Sea Paintings** were part of Marden's response to the way the sky and sea dominate the landscape. Marden had begun to paint vertical format paintings divided into light and dark halves with **Gober** (1971, New York) and **Urdan** (1970-1). The upper-lower format of the **Sea Paintings,** as with the **Hydra Paintings** of 1972, derives from Brice Marden's response to the experience of staring at the sea on the voyages he made between Greece's beautiful islands.

> *The first time we went to Greece we sailed from Bari across to Patras. I spent all the time looking out to sea and the Sea Paintings were about that... They were about looking at water.* (P, 32)

In Greece, one cannot help but be impressed by the sheer hardness and purity of the horizon line, where sky meets water: it is this pure line that bisects not only the **Sea Paintings**, but also many prints of the same period. The obviousness of the **Sea Paintings** does not detract from their power. You have an upper panel in one color and tone, which is clearly related to the sky, but poetically, and a lower half which is the sea. Sometimes the upper half is lighter, as the sky often is over the sea, as in the Saatchi Collection **Sea Painting.** This is not a rule, however: it is the **relationship** between the two panels that interests the artist. In the second Saatchi **Sea Painting**, for example, the tones and hues are very close. Hardly anything differentiates them, except that one lies above the other. As he sailed over the Adriatic and other parts of the Mediterranean, Marden would have seen many lighting changes, many different hues of blue. Sometimes the sea and sky are very close, color-wise, so that one cannot differentiate between the two, and sometimes the horizon is very misty: this is what the second **Sea Painting** depicts.

The prints related to the **Sea Paintings**, **Adriatics**, are also about the different weights and densities of the sea and sky: sometimes close, sometimes far apart. The first three of the **Adriatics** prints echo the format of the **Sea Paintings** – an upper and lower half relates to ocean and air. In these prints, the contrast between the top and bottom rectangle is very strong, even though Brice Marden modulated the contrast with foul-biting, wiping the plates and drawing on the prints. A lithograph of 1969, **Gulf** was a horizontal format image divided into two halves. The upper half is very dark, the lower half is mid-grey. **Gulf** relates directly, Marden said, to the view out of Robert Rauschenberg's window at his house in the Gulf of Mexico, at Captiva Island. The bottom edge of both rectangular blocks of color is left roughly hewn, in keeping with Marden's practice in the 1960s canvases.

GREEK, ROMAN AND EGYPTIAN ART
◆

Brice Marden in the 1970s became interested in ancient art, religion, Greek architecture, in particular, and Greek temples. This is one inspiration for the post-and-lintel and **Thira**-type images. The post-and-lintel is a 'man-made form, just very basic', Marden said.[3] Marden's art has long explored architectonics. The two and three panel paintings of the 1960s were complicated structures, concerned with the relationship between space and scale, shape and space, light and structure. This interest in fitting together panels and architecture culminated in the complex web of eighteen panels of **Thira**, which was unusual in using not only vertical but also horizontal panels.

It wasn't only the sacred architecture and art of Greece that intrigued Brice Marden. He admired, as did Mark Rothko, the Roman frescoes in Gotham's Metropolitan Museum; he later visited Pompeii. Not only the flatness and frontality of Roman painting interested Marden, but also the color, and the relation of color to space, which he began to explore rigorously in the 1970s (Roman frescoes were 'so spatial and then so flat', said Marden (in J. Lebensztejn). Roman frescoes also have that sense of the timeless that Marden strives for. Another form of ancient sacred art that Marden was concerned with were the ancient Egyptian tombs he had seen where huge rocks were rolled in front. These three cultures, the ancient Greek, Roman and Egyptian, give Marden's art a certain æsthetic weight. If you're going to allude to anything, culturally, you could do worse than go for Greek temples, Roman painting and Egyptian monumental buildings. These are part of the cultural heritage of the West, greatly vaunted by art historians.

Brice Marden was concerned with the notion of a doorway, which became one of the chief themes of **Thira** and related images. **Thira** means 'door', but it was not a doorway to Somewhere Else, the doorway as a means or entrance to another world, that concerned Marden. Rather, it was the architectonics of the doorway itself, of the doorway as a structure in its own right. **Thira** is not a doorway to Something Else, but a closed door (like the doorways and windows in Mark Rothko's murals, which drew on the false windows in Michelangelo Buonarroti's Medici Library). Similarly, in the prints in the first three of the **Five Threes**, the doorway shape is sealed. Significantly, those large boulders are sealing up the Egyptian tombs, keeping something contained.

THIRA
◆

Thira (1979-80, Musée Nationale d'Art Moderne, Paris) is the work that climaxes Brice Marden's many æsthetic concerns – with oil and wax, with multi-panel paintings, with nature, with Greece, with the relation between color and space, with mythology, and with drawing (it was an absolute delight for me to come across **Thira** in the Pompidou Centre in Paris for the first time, in 1991, on a tour of Europe by train).

The format of **Thira** is a complex interweaving of eighteen panels, which form a number of shapes, the most obvious of which is the 'T' or post-and-lintel shape, which Marden gleaned from various sources, most notably sacred Greek architecture. The word **thira** is Greek for door, but the letter 'T' is also the first letter of the word **theus** (god). Further, the T-shape recalls the headless crosses of the ancient world, the **tau** cross. In Renaissance art Christ and the two thieves are sometimes shown being crucified on **tau** crosses. Marden himself adjusted his color so that the cross shape would not be so obvious: he knew how it would be perceived. Besides, there are other shapes in **Thira** of a similar significance. For example, the emphasis on the cross shape inevitably gives **Thira** a Christian connotation. Some art critics have linked **Thira** with Golgotha and Calvary.[4] Certainly, in one interpretation, the sombreness of **Thira** is indisputable. It seems to be a return to the solemnity of the 1960s monochrome canvases. One can see how much red there is in **Thira** for example: like the second and third paintings in the **Annunciation Series, Thira** is very red. And red, growing into black, is one of the main color frames of Renaissance depictions of the **Crucifixion**. The reddish hue in Renaissance **Crucifixions** not only occurs in the bleeding wounds of Christ. One sees it in the apocalyptic skies, which look like brooding clouds moments before a storm. If one studies Simone Martini's **Entombment** (Berlin), **Pietàs** by Rogier van der Weyden or **Crucifixions** by Tintoretto, one finds that dour, brownish sky that echoes the tragedy occurring in the foreground. At one glance, Marden's **Thira** may too partake of this gloomy sort of **Crucifixion** atmosphere. There are blacks and reds enough in **Thira** to account for a Golgotha setting. The coloration when combined with the crosses makes the Christian Passion reading convincing (Marden confirmed that he was thinking of 'the imagery of the Crucifixion', of a tall cross and two smaller crosses [M. Poirier, 1985, 61]). **Thira** does look like a central **tau** cross and two smaller **tau** crosses on either side, echoing exactly the configuration of Christ and the two thieves in the **New Testament** and in many a Renaissance painting (in Jan van Eyck's **Crucifixion** in the Metropolitan Museum, for example, which also features the crucified ones on **tau** crosses). Further, Brice Marden had worked on the **Annunciation Series** before painting **Thira,** so he was

clearly familiar with Christian themes. Marden was also developing on a commission for Basle cathedral to produce some stained
glass during this late 1970s period.

What about a Greek Orthodox reading of **Thira**? That is, seeing
Thira as partaking not of the Catholic and Neoplatonic Italy of the
Renaissance, nor of the Protestantism of Early Netherlandish
painting, but the much more severe, demanding, passionate and
ascetic Eastern orthodox form of Christianity. Entering Greek
churches, the faithful do not simply go to a pew and sit down,
they kiss icons, they kiss bones and relics, they genuflect and
kneel and bow many times. While Italian Catholic followers may
seem fervent, they seem positively restrained and demure
compared to the Greek Orthodox laity.

These are loose generalizations, but they may help to
understand the severity of Brice Marden's **Thira**, **Number Two** and
the related prints. **Thira** may partake of that powerful blend of
Christianity and paganism, Catholicism and the Classical world,
that one finds in a filmmaker such as Pier Paolo Pasolini. Pasolini's vision of the ancient world, in his films of Classic Greek
texts, is harsh, dusty, sunbaked, passionate and violent. Perhaps
Marden's Greek paintings hope to evoke a similar world of sun,
rock, myth, sea and desire. Pasolini's movies combine a rigorous
interpretation of ancient Greek drama with a pagan worldview
that has not entirely jettisoned some Catholic sentiments. The
world of Pasolini's **Oedipus Rex** and **Medea** may offer a parallel
to Brice Marden's Greek paintings – not only **Thira**, but also the
Sea Paintings, **Hydra**, **Lethykos**, **Grove Group**, **Adriatics**, **To Corfu**
and others.

It is worth mentioning also that Pier Paolo Pasolini made the most powerful version of the Christian story, taken straight from the **Gospels**. Filmed on a tiny budget, with many amateur actors, **The Gospel According to Matthew** (1964) is a searing and highly moving portrayal of the key moments of Western religion. Brice Marden has nowhere attained similar Pasolinian moments of emotional intensity – and neither has it been his intention to be so melodramatic. Pasolini's genius, though, was to take the melodramas of the **Gospels**, which we have seen a billion times before, and make them seem fresh and alive, as if they were happening now.

Brice Marden's paintings operate quite differently from movies, but there are common moods and themes in the art of Marden and Pier Paolo Pasolini. One might also mention other filmmakers in connection with Marden, such as Michelangelo Antonioni, whose films (**The Passenger, L'Avventura** and **Identification of a Woman**) are full of empty spaces in a style familiar from 1960s Minimalism. Of all mainstream filmmakers Antonioni – and Jean-Luc Godard – most approximate to the sculpture and painting of the mid-1960s Minimal era (one also thinks of Ingmar Bergman, Luis Buñuel, Marco Ferreri, Andrei Tarkovsky and Roman Polanski in connection with Brice Marden. Godard's movies, meanwhile, are the perfect embodiment of the Pop Art, comicbook sensibility of the 1960s).

Yet another reading of Brice Marden's **Thira** might not discount the Christian, tragic interpretation, but look to the pre-Christian world of ancient Greece. If we remember that Marden was much concerned in the 1970s with the natural world, with natural colors and forms, then the colors of **Thira** – reds, browns, greens, blacks, light blues – take on a different meaning. Series of paintings such as the **Moon, Grove Group, Hydra** and **Sea Paintings** all started with colors found in nature. Remember that Marden spoke of sitting under olive groves and observing the trees, or gazing at the sea. The colors in **Thira**, then, may have more of a natural than a spiritual or symbolic basis. Even so, **Thira**'s colors **are** perplexing. You have to stare at **Thira** for a while before you understand the complex interrelationships of the colors.

Here's a brief summary of **Thira**'s color scheme: there are three groups of panels which together form a vertical rectangle of panels. There are seven panels in the right and left hand groups, four in the central group. So far so good. Each T-shape is enclosed by a single color: green on the left, red on the right. Inside this enclosure is the **tau** cross or 'post-and-lintel': in red on the left, in near-black on the right. On either side of the column or upright stem of each **tau** cross are complimentary colors (though not complimentary in the technical sense of the color wheel). On the left group of panels, a blue-black color lies either side of the mid-red **tau** cross; in the right hand group of panels, an earth brown.

So far so good. Then the colors become complicated. For example, the mid-red of the left hand **tau** cross becomes the lintel of the central group. This would not present any problems, but this mid-red abuts the slightly darker red that surrounds the right hand **tau** cross: usually Brice Marden, in his brighter, deeper paintings of the 1970s does not have adjacent panels with very similar color values. So this choice for the lintel of the central **tau** cross is odd.

On either side of the central vertical pillar, which is a light blue, are two colors which pick up from the surrounds of the two

outside **tau** crosses. This is a traditional structure of color
harmony: the slightly lighter green of the right hand side of the
central group, for example, clearly relates to the mid-green that
surrounds the left hand **tau** cross, and vice versa for the slightly
darker red on the left hand side of the central pillar.

This messy description is wholly inadequate to describe the
impact of the colors in Brice Marden's **Thira**. There are economies
of harmony and conflict taking place, of revolving colors and
spiralling colors, of circularity and repetition. The movements the
colors in **Thira** create can be read as linear or static, circular or
open, depending on a number of factors.

One structure is clear, however: **Thira** is essentially based on the
Renaissance triptych: the structure of the left and right hand
groups mirror each other, just as in a triptych by anyone from Fra
Angelico to Max Beckmann. The central panel is quite different,
although it reprises the post-and-lintel/ **tau** cross shape. But it is in
this central group that we end up, after journeying around the
wings, as is usual in a triptych. If there is a doorway to something
in Marden's **Thira**, this is where it will be situated, in the central
group. It is significant, then, that the central vertical panel of **Thira**
is a pale blue, suggesting distance, the sky, infinity – a beyond, in
short.

Thira's colors suggest not only nature but also the elemental,
flat colors of frescoes: red, green, brown, blue. Other critics have
suggested that **Thira**'s 'fiercely polychrome' quality may refer to
Greek temples (S. Bann, W, 14). It is worth recalling, when
considering Brice Marden's love of ancient architecture, that
temples and statues were multi-colored. Instead of white marble
and stone, Greek art was colorful. This is something of a shock, so

used are we to thinking of ancient Greek art as a cool near-white. This whiteness fits in with the view of the ancient Greeks as seekers after purity and philosophical perfection. Somehow the thought of multicolored temples and statues is too garish. It doesn't square with the view of the Classic era as one of sophistication in the arts and sciences.

The relation of the painting **Thira** to Greek architecture and to the polychromatic nature of the architecture makes sense: **Thira** is if nothing else a supremely architectural painting. The very physicality of slotting together those eighteen panels so that they would not only fit snugly but work æsthetically was a difficult task. **Thira** asserts its physical presence through the fact of those eighteen panels, which one critic likens to stones which when piled up together create a wall (N. Hale, 152). Seeing **Thira** as a wall of stone goes some way in explaining its impenetrable nature. It is a painting that calls for a certain amount of work in order to fully perceive everything in it.

Another way of looking at **Thira** as a blocked doorway or stone wall is to think of the colors and light which are reflected off walls and architectural structures. **Thira** is seen then as an abstract portrait of the Greek landscape. All of the connotations that cluster around the ancient landscape of Greece – purity, harshness, fatality, tragedy, joy, ruggedness – can be read into **Thira**'s difficult array of black, green and red.

What about the mythological aspects of **Thira**? We have already seen how Brice Marden used Robert Graves' mythopœia in constructing his **Moon Paintings, Five Threes** and **For Hera**. In **Thira** one can, if one wishes, see a host of mythological allusions. One can recall the gods and goddesses of the ancient world, and the extraordinary, cruel, violent, aggressive, tender and insane things they did; one can recall the Minoan myths associated with the legendary island of Thira (called Santorini today) and its associations with the Atlantis myth; one can recall the myths of Homer, or Mycenæ, or Knossos.

Brice Marden's **Thira** is compatible with any amount of mythological metaphors, for it is open and abstract enough for that. **Thira** fits in with the view of the ancient Greek landscape as cruel and harsh, but also beautiful and magical. **Thira** can be seen like the Greek temple, as a structure which modulates the cruelty as well as the tenderness of ancient Greece. **Thira** gives the rocky, mythic space of Greece a classical order. It organizes the conflict and heat, the fatality and despair of ancient Greece into a series of precise architectonic forms.

But all this talk of the 'stark severity' of the ancient Greek elements of Brice Marden's **Thira** (N. Hale, 153) does not cancel out a tragic, fatal Christian reading. If one recalls the austerity and asceticism of the Early Christian Church, as practised by the fervent initiates and devotees of the era between the time of St Paul and St Augustine in the Near East, this accords with the harshness of Marden's mythic Greece.

What one keeps returning to with **Thira**, **Coda,** the **Numbers** and **Elements Series** and the related imagery of the late 1970s/ early 1980s, is the way Brice Marden transformed his response to ancient and contemporary Greece into a rigorously executed series of rectangles and harmonizing colors. For, although **Thira** may be a sounding board for any number of explorations into Christianity, Greek mythology, numerology, sacred architecture, and so on, it is also a painting by a Postminimal New Yorker.

That is, it remains a particular kind of cultural artifact, subject, as any artwork is, to all manner of æsthetic, social, political and ideological factors.

Paintings such as **Thira,** the **Numbers Series,** the **Elements Series** and **Green (Earth)** are characterized by the artist as 'repressed and angry' works. 'I like to think of them as being very aggressive', he said (M. Poirier, 1985, 52). It seems that the depression of the mid-1960s was not completely shaken off, and periodically returned to haunt Marden. In the early 1980s, for instance, Marden left his wife and family to live for a time in his studio on Bond Street. In his notebooks for the period of the **Thira, Number Two, Elements, Coda** and **Green (Earth)** paintings (1979-1984), Marden wrote:

> *Black – death, destruction, humiliation/ red – suffering of Christ, the cup, the cross of suffering, the wine, John, Jesus as hanged man, the figure of a hanged or crucified man.* (ib., 61)

Another **Thira**-type painting is **Number Two** (1983-4, collection: Martin Margulies, Miami). Frontality, non-illusionism, flatness and formalism are emphasized. There are some six colors here, a system of complementaries. Thus, the T-shape on the right is in mid-red; outside the T-form on the left is a darker red. In the middle post and lintel, a deep violet; outside the right-hand post and lintel, ultramarine. Brice Marden orchestrates his colors according to a musical, formal plan. Light-toned colors are complimented by darker tones in the adjacent panels. No colors are allowed to run continuously across a number of panels, though behind the central purple T-shape is a bright yellow, which was used to such effect in the **Annunciation Series**.

Number One (1983-4, Whitney, New York) is another of the large, multi-panel **Thira**-type paintings that Brice Marden was working on during 1983 and 1984 (such as the **Elements Series, Green (Earth),** and others). With its twelve panels (as with **Green (Earth)**), **Number One** is nearly as complicated, structurally, as the 18-panel **Thira**. **Number One** is among the darkest of the **Thira** era paintings, with over half (seven) of the panels very dark tonally (in blacks and ultramarines). The reds, too, are severe, especially those in the right-hand **tau** shape. Two central panels, though, stave off the darkness that threatens to consume **Number One**: the mid-red and yellow of the central uprights of the **tau** crosses in the centre of the left-hand groups of panels. Although these paintings are 'aggressive', as Marden accepted, he did not let them become wholly consumed by darkness. Actually, the **Thira** paintings are amongst his brightest works. Only one painting appears relentlessly 'negative' or 'depressed', in the old, 1960s Marden sense, and that is **Green (Earth)** . But even this painting is actually (partly) about the fecund powers of the Earth, its dark soil and green plants.

The post and lintel multi-panel format of **Thira, Numbers One** and **Two,** the **Elements Series, Coda, Green (Earth)** and other paintings proved to be loose enough for any number of serial variations. Brice Marden could vary the hues and tones **ad infinitum**, it seemed. The severe shapes of the rectangular panels were a rigorous framework to hold down the explorations of color and tone.

Elements II (1981-82, Stedelijk Museum) is just one **tau** cross shape, composed of four panels. The colors relate to Brice Marden's alchemical concept of the four elements (fire, air, earth, water): blue, earth-brown, dark green and mustard yellow. Though alchemically-allusive, these hues in **Elements II** are kept firmly earthbound, closely tied to colors found in the natural world. The shape of the **tau**-cross is emphasized by Marden placing the two warmer colors (ochre and yellow) on either side of the viridian panel which forms the upright of the cross. **Elements I** has three vertical panels (red, blue, yellow) capped by a horizontal green (earth) panel. The colors in **Elements IV** (1983-4, New York) are the vivid, near-primary colors of the **Red, Yellow, Blue Series**: the red, yellow and blue appear twice, but modulated each time. On the left is a mid-red, which is repeated but lightened a little in the fourth panel from the left. In amongst the bright primary colors in **Elements IV** there are the colors of the **Thira**-type paintings: dark blues and olive greens. The presence of these darker, earthier colors moves **Elements IV** on from the more joyful exchanges in the **Red, Yellow, Blue Series**.

 Frieze II (1982, M. & J. Ovitz) is a large work (145 inches wide) of oil on paper, mounted on Shoji screens. Essentially, **Frieze II** works out another variation on the **Thira**-type painting. The same colors as used in the **Elements Series** appear: mustard yellows, earth-browns and ochres, olive greens, azures. The symmetrical design at first confers a uniformity upon the **tau**-cross shapes in **Frieze II**, as shapes reflect across the central axis. However, Brice Marden's color combinations are never merely symmetrical. As one follows a color across **Frieze II** – the sepia or brown, say – one finds that Marden is modulating his colors each time they appear, setting them against slightly different greens or blues. The exquisite architectural form of the **Thira** paintings, such as **Frieze II, Elements, Green (Earth)** and **Coda**, then, offers a solid structure upon which Marden develops his most sophisticated arrangements of color.

☆

Two paintings represent the end of Brice Marden's multi-panel oil paintings of the type begun in the late 1960s: **Coda** and **Green (Earth)**. **Coda** (1983-4, Philadelphia Museum of Art) is an unusual format for Marden: two small **tau** cross motifs are set side by side above four large vertical uprights. The irregular combination of shapes and sizes recalls the shaped canvases and panels of Sean Scully. The painting appears large, even though it is 77 inches high (compared to **Green (Earth)** , which's a horizontal format, is 84 inches high, and **Thira,** which's 96 inches tall). The colors of **Coda** are extremely positive, the opposite of the very subdued, nay, solemn, coloration of **Green (Earth)** . In **Coda** Marden reprises the colors of the **Red, Yellow, Blue Series**, which he used also in the **Numbers** and **Elements Series**. Red, yellow, blue and green are used three times each: once each in the four large uprights, and twice each in the **tau** crosses. **Coda** is not altogether success-ful in its combinations of color and shape and scale. The mixture of two shapes of panels, the upper and lower forms, produces an irregular outline, destroying the familiar (and sacred) Brice Marden rectangle.

Green (Earth) (1983-4, private collection) is one of Brice Marden's most severe and solemn paintings. There is light green here, but most of the colors are dark and sombre. **Green (Earth)** is the dark, opaque flipside to **Coda**'s primary colors. Marden wrote of the earth: 'Look at the earth. Stare at it for 42 hours and see if anything grows out of it. Then try to figure out why.' Yet **Green (Earth)** is not a 'negative', somewhat life-denying painting, like the 'depressed' works of the 1960s.

CHAPTER *8*

Prints and Drawings

THROUGHOUT HIS career Brice Marden has produced prints –
lithographs, etchings, screenprints. The prints echo many of the
themes and formal considerations of the oil and wax paintings, as
one might expect. Before the development into loose, open
calligraphic imagery of the 1980s, most of Marden's prints were
based on solid blocks of ink, mostly in rectangles, just like his
paintings with their reliance on the rectangle and the 'smooth'
and 'constant' field of color.

Early prints, of the mid-1960s, such as the screenprints of the
Lana series (1966), closely parallel paintings of the period (such as
Last Dylan Study, Nico's Painting and **Plumb II**). They are blocks
of grey with the bottom edge left open. **Gulf** (discussed earlier)
echoes the horizontal format paintings divided into two halves of

the late 1960s. The eight etchings in **Ten Days** (1971) offer many parallels with the paintings. The second print, for example, is a small vertical format etching (the image is 21.6 x 10.6 in), is divided into two tones; the upper one very dark, the lower one nearly white. The format recalls paintings such as **Smith** (1971) and also the **Sea Paintings** and the **Hydra Series**, which divided the area into two halves. The fourth print in the **Ten Days** edition is a dense grid, which became more and more a favourite formal device for Brice Marden. Many of his prints are based on the grid, sometimes very dark and dense, such as in **Ten Days, Untitled** (1973-9), while others were very loose grids, such as in the prints **Painting Study I** (1974), **Grid I** (1971), or the eighth of **Ten Days**. Often the grid prints and drawings were part of extended series, such as the **Shape Book** (1973-5, Konrad Fischer, Düsseldorf) or **Five Studies** (1978).

Some of the most successful grid-based prints were the **Adriatics** portfolio. The first three of these seven etchings had the vertical sea-sky format (discussed above), related to the Greek **Sea Paintings** and the **Hydra Paintings**. The first print has diagonal lines drawn across the upper, white half, which could be linked with the brilliant skies of Greece, the shafts of light slicing down out of the void. The grids of the four etchings of the **Adriatics** are not absolutely geometrically precise: Marden allows inconsistencies and odd marks to modulate the severity of the grid.

Brice Marden's grid is a formal device which allows him to explore other formal aspects of printing. It is something to pin the formal exploration on. Thus, instead of having a thick black and a faint white upper and lower half to his vertical rectangle, Marden experiments with a closely knit grid underneath or on top of a looser grid.

For Helen (1970, Helen Harrington Marden) is related to the **Grove Group** paintings, with its tripartite structure and dense color. Indeed, this is one of Brice Marden's most impenetrable drawings, where the wax crayon, beeswax and graphite has been rubbed vigorously into the surface of the paper, so hard that only the narrow bottom edge shows any let-up from the coating of blackness. Even the **Grove Group** drawings (such as **Grove Group III** (1972) and **Grove Group IV** (1972-3, both Crispo Collection), are very dense – **Grove Group IV** being particularly impenetrable.

Some of Brice Marden's drawings and prints use two colors: after Marden made the original etching or sketch in black ink he went over it, often with gouache, often in pale blue or violet (as in **Grace Notes**, 1992-3), the **Hemlock** series (1992-3), **Aphrodite Study, The Virgins** and the **Tu Fu Dog** etchings of 1991-3. Marden often painted on top of his grid etchings, too, adding drips and colors and anomalies to the rigid black lattices.

TILES AND GRIDS
◆

Brice Marden has been using the grid for a long time. It is one of the key structures of modern, abstract art, from the art of Kasimir Malevich and Piet Mondrian onwards. Marden acknowledged the influence of Mondrian, and called one of his **Tiles** prints a 'boogie woogie' work, after Mondrian's famous **Broadway Boogie**

Woogie. After the post-and-lintel structures of **Thira** and related prints and paintings, Marden moved into open squares, with bands of black lines, crisscrossing. Still the rectangle was predominant: at this point (late 1970s, early 1980s), Marden had not moved into the loose curves and spirals of his calligraphic period. The **Mirabelle Drawings** (1978-9, New York) veer from open vertical forms to densely layered shapes. Some of the **Tiles** prints (1979) are very open, with just a few vertical and horizontal lines on top of white; others are very dense, with lines layered on top of lines. These prints are built up gradually, with Marden drawing one thin line after another until a pattern of multiple lines is produced.

In the **Focus** prints (1979), which is a portfolio of five aquatint etchings on handmade Twinrocker paper, the door motif recurs: they are frames and boxes, one inside the other, which Brice Marden regarded as almost 'theatrical settings' (P, 133). In the **Focus** prints theatricality is heightened by the impression of a doorway or central space in white surrounded by the darkened wings or drapes or proscenium arch of a theatre. In some of Marden's late 1979 prints there are large areas of white deliberately spotted and dirtied. At this time, Marden was experimenting with drawing with sticks of wood, dipped in sugar solution. The combination of the sugarlift and foul biting technique gives the prints a handmade, intuitive feel. They are not pristine images of black lines on crisp, clean white Somerset satin paper. As with the 1960s monochrome paintings, Brice Marden leaves spaces in the paint area where the artwork's manufacture is apparent. He wants the viewer to see the accidents and spontaneity of art making. Thus, the prints have uneven shading, blacks that are not

completely solid, and lines that break and veer from being precisely straight. In particular, as with so many contemporary
painters, Marden allows a certain imprecision around the edges of
his works.

The **Hydra Group** drawings of 1979 reworked the doorway/
Thira motif, again strictly tied to a grid. The oil on paper **Hydra
Group** drawings/ paintings employ colors quite different from the
Thira paintings, however, and the doorway motif is dominant,
not the post-and-lintel motif of the **Thira** paintings. **Hydra Group
V** reveals the post-and-lintel pattern, but drawings such as **Hydra
Group III** and **Hydra Group IX** (all Thomas Ammann, Zurich),
explore the motif of a doorway set in walls – or, rather, a rectangle
inside another rectangle, for Marden is never explicitly figurative.

The **Melia Drawings** (1980-81, Matthew Marks, New York),
named after Brice Marden's second daughter, explored both the
Marden grid and the doorway/ **Thira** motif. Marden used gouache
as well as ink in these drawings – the gouache paint gave him a
thick white and black which added a new texture to the spindly
and blotchy quality of the black ink. The **Melia Group** drawings
were made on different colored paper (off-white, grey and pink)
upon which Marden drew a vertical rectangle which he divided in
a number of ways, concentrating on the central horizontal line,
and the thickness and weight of the outer edges. In most of the
Melia Group one diagonal line appears, one spindly diagonal
amongst the fine and blotchy horizontals and verticals.

Other grid drawings and prints included a closely-packed
Untitled of 1980, where the lines are so closely drawn together
they overlap (in an ink drawing over an etching). In **Painting Study
III** (1980, collection: Mirabelle Marden), the ink (in black, beige

and violet), is allowed to drip and smudge. A number of drawings, such as the **Card Drawing** series, **New Year Addenda I** and **Untitled Postcard Drawing** , employ existing images (in this case, postcards and printed cards).

The **Masking Drawings** of the mid-1980s were related to the Basle commission. In these works Brice Marden developed further his tendency towards openness and spontaneity. No longer were the edges and areas of color meticulously separate: Marden encouraged colors to bleed and merge. Indeed, the **Masking Drawings** take their title from the paper that the artist used to mask one color from another when he was making his single color multi-panel paintings. In the **Masking Drawings** (such as **Masking Drawing 5**, 1984, collection: the artist), Marden employed a number of media (oil, ink, gouache and graphite) to obscure and mask the black grid. Some of the lines blur the grid, others re-inforce it, but in doing so re-draw it, as with the **Melia Group**, the **Painting Studies** and the various **Untitled** drawing-etchings. Even so, the grid is always underneath there somewhere. In **Basle Drawing** (1983, collection: the artist), blocks of color augment the grid (red, lilac, yellow), but the grid remains pre-dominant.

One of the most densely layered and worked of the grid and ink drawings is **4 and 3 Drawing** (1979-81, P. Schrager), which is a thick cluster of red, green and black horizontal and vertical lines. What is striking about **4 and 3 Drawing**, though, is the number of 'mistakes' that Brice Marden has allowed to stay in the final picture: there are at last six sizeable ink blotches, and many smaller ones. These ink accidents disrupt finally the primacy of the grid, redrawing the rigidity of the horizontal and vertical web.

Many times Marden reworked earlier pieces. The **Card Drawings**, for example, reworked earlier printed cards of one of Marden's grid drawings. On top of the cards, as with other grid works, Marden added more and more lines, sometimes allowing the ink to drip and smudge the printed piece.

The paintings Brice Marden made inspired by his Basle cathedral commission comprised of strident vertical and diagonal lines drawn over neutral backgrounds. Despite the introduction of the 'dynamic' diagonal, the Basle paintings remained anchored in the formal rigidity of the grid. The Basle cathedral commission required 4 sets of circular arch windows, 6 Gothic rose windows and 5 choir windows. Marden found the commission inspiring (even though it was not fulfilled – the sponsors cancelled the project). Marden explored the alchemical allusions of four colors (red, blue, yellow, green), and also employed the symbolism of the **Book of Revelation**. The need for transparency required that Marden rethink his usual opaque surface of oil and wax. The new transparency is apparent in paintings such as the last of the **Thira**-type works, **Coda**.

One group of paintings related to the Basle commission (the **Sketch** series) incorporated Brice Marden's motifs of the grid, the plane, the relation of two halves, and planar geometry. **Sketch I** (1983, Edelman, Switzerland) kept to the horizontal and verticals of the grid, with one strip of color moving into a single plane of color. At this point, **Sketch I** was not much of a departure from the usual Marden motifs of multi-panel paintings with a single color on each panel. **Sketch III** (1983, private collection), how-ever, introduced the dynamic diagonal line, and looked towards the 'calligraphic' works of the second half of the 1980s. The two

Basle **Window Paintings** (both 1983) employed the wide, horizontal format of the **Thira**-type **Frieze II**. The rectangles, each with a different colored background, recalled the single-color rectangles of the **Thira** group. But on top of this background (in the 4 alchemical colors, red, green, yellow, blue). Brice Marden layered marks horizontally and diagonally. This was very different from the paintings up to **Thira**, the **Elements** and **Numbers** series. These diagonal marks, with their fuzzy edges and drips, did away with the relentless flatness of Marden's monochrome multi-panel works. Suddenly there was foreground and background, of marks 'floating' upon a ground. Instantly, there was a return to Renaissance space, with its perspectival illusions of three dimensions. In **First Window Painting** (private collection) and **Second Window Painting** (collection: the artist), color was no longer primary; marks and gestures became crucial, and would preoccupy Marden in all his subsequent painting.

In three works of 1985 – **Untitled (for Helen)** (collection: Helen Harrington Marden), **Window Study Green and Red** (N. & J. Bickford), and **Yellow Window Study** (private collection) – the movement into the 'Oriental', 'calligraphic' mode is almost complete. The grid is still there, but color has become secondary to the gestural marks of the diagonal and horizontal lines, made with a single brush stroke drawn across the surface, quite different from the texture of the oil and wax canvases, where the surfaces were smooth, with no brush marks visible.

Brice Marden made some paintings on marble, fragments of Greek marble, which constituted a direct contact with Greece. The marble paintings (**Marble #12, Marble #4, Marble #13**, 1981-4, all private collection), imposed the Marden grid and planar geometry onto irregular pieces of marble. The irregularities of the marble chunks were incorporated into the design – Marden drew around the jagged edges of the marble.

GLYPHS, COUPLETS, IDEOGRAMS AND OTHER 'ORIENTAL' MOTIFS
◆

I'm trying to make a glyph for paradise.

Brice Marden, 1983 (in PD, 41)

Glyphs (1986, private collection) was a cluster of twelve 'glyphs', arranged in four columns of three glyphs. The grid still underpinned the painting, but the looseness of the black and creamy-yellow gestures is the most obvious element of the work. **February** (1986, private collection) was also based on the grid, but the openness of the brushmarks is vigorous, recalling Willem de Kooning, very much a departure from the **Numbers, Coda** and **Green (Earth)** paintings of two years before. Brice Marden still put his work into groups. One group of 'Oriental' oil paintings on linen was the **Untitled** series of 1986-7. The vaguely triangular glyphs were still present, as in **Glyphs**, but Marden began to color in some of the glyphs, and the spaces they made as they intertwined. He was moving further into a semi-abstraction, evoking illusory spaces, of one plane on top of another – as in **Untitled 2** (1986, Carnegie Museum of Art), **Untitled 3** (A. Gund & D. Shapiro) and **Untitled 4** (1986-7, Dar Reedy).

The series just given numbers as titles were also vertical format oils on linen (this time the calligraphic **Numbers**, painted in 1987-88, were all 84 by 60 inches). Brice Marden began to interweave different colors as trails of brushstrokes. In **2 (Dialog)** (H. & R. Goldenberg), three motifs (in red, blue and dark green) are placed beside each other, while a large, complex grey motif is layered on top of them. Behind this already complicated spatial weave is a light blue glyph on the right. There is a shallow sense of depth: the picture is still distinctly 'abstract', a series of interwoven lines, but the glyphs overlap and intertwine, giving at least three of four planes to the painting. **3** (Baltimore Museum of Art) is simpler, spatially, though the (upper) white glyph is one of Marden's most complex. In **4 (Bone)** (Helen Harrington Marden) an unusual cream-yellow hue provides the background – this color recalls parchment or aged paper, and Marden has worked at the background vigorously, before lacing a grey and dried blood color glyph on top. One can see the places where Marden changed his mind, and painted over the pattern of the glyph. Other paintings in this **Numbers** series employed layers of glyphs in simple colors (yellow, red, grey, black), without coloring in the spaces the motifs made: **9 (Air)** (private collection), **10 (Dialog 2)** (Edward Lee Family Collection), and **11 (to Leger)** (L. & H. Macklowe).

The **Couplet Series** (1988-89) took their departure point from Chinese poetry, and are the works of Brice Marden's that look most like Chinese ideograms. The comparison is heightened by the choice of a faint grey-white ground, which gives the works a lightness which is aided by the linen support. **Diagrammed Couplet I** (collection: the artist) might pass as Chinese calligraphy at a cursory glance: closer inspection reveals the looseness and abstraction of Marden's motifs. **Couplet I** (Sammlung Marx, Berlin) links two glyphs together in a dual color dance. Subsequent **Couplet** paintings (**Couplet II** and **Couplet IV,** both private coll- ections), added more colors to the basic pattern of two inter- connected motifs (blue, yellow, red, green).

This increasing complexity of interwoven glyphs found its apotheosis in the **Cold Mountain Series**, the sixth painting of which was, like **Thira**, one of Brice Marden's most complex compositions (even though **Cold Mountain 6 (Bridge)** employed three main colors in the motifs: blue, green and black). In a way, the **studies** for the 'Oriental'/ 'calligraphic' paintings were more successful than the oil on linen paintings. Due to the small scale, in the ink and gouache studies and sketches it looks as if Marden was able to control the movement of the stick and the brush easier than in the large scale canvases. Thus, studies such as **Couplet Painting Study II** (1988, collection: the artist) are more impressive than the final painting.

☆

Around the mid-1980s, Brice Marden's art became increasingly concerned with Oriental art, with Chinese calligraphy and Zen Buddhism's (non-)imagery. Print series included the **Etchings For Rexroth** and the **Cold Mountain Series**. These concerns are discussed in the next chapter.

CHAPTER *9*

Brice Marden Goes East

BRICE MARDEN'S art has always had its 'Oriental' component. Much of Abstract Expressionism, Minimal and contemporary art has affinities with Zen Buddhism and Taoism – the exaltation of emptiness, the integration of chaos and void, the flatness of Oriental art and those huge flat areas of color in the art of Barnett Newman, Robert Motherwell and Mark Rothko. Marden, in his use of Oriental-style calligraphic motifs and glyphs, is continuing a tradition of exploring aspects of Eastern philosophy begun by the Abstract Expressionists (although Western artists had been exploring the Orient for hundreds of years previous to Jackson Pollock, Motherwell and Newman). Marden's Oriental philosophy has affinities with famous Eastern figures such as Matsuo Basho and Chuang-tzu. Basho, an important Oriental poet, wrote:

Go to the pine if you want to learn about the pine, or to the bamboo if you want to learn about the bamboo. And in doing so, you must leave your subjective preoccupation with yourself.[1]

Makoto Ueda glosses what Basho says thus: '[f]or learn means to enter into the object. Perceive its delicate life and feel its feelings.'[2] These notions of searching for the 'essence' are absolutely in tune with the æsthetics of 1960s Minimalists, Carl Andre, Robert Smithson, Dan Flavin and Donald Judd. Brice Marden speaks in exactly the same terms of trying to find the 'essence' of nature.

Another key thinker and writer of the Orient, the Chinese Taoist mystic, Chuang-tzu (the 'Groucho Marx of Taoism' as Lawrence Durrell calls him), wrote:

Leap into the boundless and make it your home.[3]

This statement perfectly describes the artist's act of faith and risk, which is so essential for good artistic creations. As Søren Kirkegaard said, without risk, life is not worth living. Again, these quasi-Existentialist/ Taoist notions of risk are perfectly in tune with 1960s Minimalism (and 1950s Abstract Expressionism), and Brice Marden's art. Chuang-tzu also wrote

Look into that closed room, the empty chamber where brightness is born! Fortune and blessing gather where there is stillness.[4]

Brice Marden's works seem to work towards this kind of Oriental stillness and brightness.

☆

Photographs taken in Brice Marden's studio between March,

1992 and April, 1993 showed many long paintbrushes of different thicknesses: some of them two feet long. Beside half-squeezed tubes of paint were bundles of sticks, some of them thin, mere twigs, some of them half an inch thick. On a piece of paper, four large sea shells were arranged (Marden collects shells).

Photographs of Brice Marden at work in the 1980s and 1990s – dressed, as usual, in black (well, this *is* New York), in his American studio, or in Greece – depict the artist standing well back from the wall on which a smallish piece of paper is pinned. It is a most unusual pose for a painter: he crouches, leaning forward, left hand on his knee, the other grasping a five foot-long stick, the forefinger extending along the stick, to control it. The painter's eyes are some six feet from his painting or drawing as he paints it. This is the distance one might step back from a work to view it as a whole, but this is the distance Marden prefers to work from as he makes the piece.

I, II, III, 1, 2, 3, 4, AND *UNTITLED*
◆

Though the new 'calligraphic', 'Oriental' paintings of the 1980s onwards did not seem to have the gestures towards plangency and monumentality of the multi-panel oil and wax works of the 1970s, up to **Thira**, this did not deter Brice Marden, who pro-ceeded to make more paintings, it seems, than at any other time in his career. Some of the most 'Oriental' of Marden's works are

the print series **Untitled, I, II, III** and **1, 2, 3, 4**. These were all
screenprints, made in 1983. They consist of open squares created
with a wide brush. In contrast to the grids, these prints are some
of Marden's most simple and reduced images. Apart from the
bold, black open squares there is little else in the prints.

The simplicity, though, is deceptive. Brice Marden introduces a
number of variations into **Untitled, I, II, III** and **1, 2, 3, 4** which
modulate the basic structure. In **Untitled**, for example, Marden
thins out the brushstroke, and pulls them over the edge of the
square. In **I, II, III**, he again pulls some of the sides of the squares
beyond the geometry of the normal square. Further, there are
vertical lines which bisect the squares, which form two compart-
ments of vertical rectangles, echoing again the **Thira**-type doorway
image. In **1, 2, 3, 4** Marden draws a narrow square around the
thicker open square. These two squares are set within a larger
rectangular space of a dark tone.

Brice Marden's **Untitled, I, II, III** and **1, 2, 3, 4** recall a number
of contemporary artists' work. Jasper Johns, for example, has made
densely-shaded sketches, where the crosshatching is thick and
makes deep black squares and rectangles. The five-foot black
squares of Ad Reinhardt and other Abstract Expressionists, such as
Franz Kline, are also obvious parallels with Marden's **Untitled, I,
II, III** and **1, 2, 3, 4.** Going further back, Kasimir Malevich's red
and black squares are obvious ancestors of contemporary
abstraction.[5]

Some contemporary black squares, such as those of Jasper Johns
and Brice Marden, recall the magic squares of the Renaissance
alchemist Robert Fludd (1574-1637). Fludd produced a small
black square, a mass of lines and crosshatching which has **Et sic**

infinitum written along each of the four sides. Fludd's magic square is an alchemical statement on the original chaos before life began, but it is also a beautiful object in its own right. The black magic squares are seen now by critics as forerunners of modern abstraction – as precursors of Malevich, Piet Mondrian, Johns and Marden.

The alchemical/ cosmological/ Fludd connection is one (Western) parallel with Brice Marden's open black squares in **Untitled, I, II, III** and **1, 2, 3, 4.** Another is Oriental calligraphy, in particular Zen Buddhist imagery. Zen philosophy is of course distinctly non-representational, like the art of Islam. Part of the point of Zen Buddhism, as with Islam, is that the divine or numinous or **isness** cannot be depicted. The **thatness** or **dasein** of Oriental mysticism is beyond the grasp of words or images. Hence the Zen **koan**, and the compactness of Zen **haiku** poems. Hence the impulse in Oriental art to throw the viewer outwards, into the void. Behind the mountains and trees of Chinese painting is the sky, the void. Similarly, behind Chinese calligraphy is the void.

Brice Marden's open black squares in **Untitled, I, II, III** and **1, 2, 3, 4** echo this preoccupation in Zen Buddhism with emptiness. Marden's black squares are wholly abstract shapes; they are black squares only; they are geometry as pure abstraction. In Zen Buddhism there is a 'test' or technique of drawing a circle. One judges how far along the path of enlightenment the initiate is by their ability to draw a circle. However, the point is not to think about drawing the circle consciously, but simply to draw, uninhibited, unself-consciously, directly. Marden's **Untitled, I, II, III** and **1, 2, 3, 4** screenprints, then, may be seen as a Western equivalent of this Eastern philosophic practice. It is quite in

keeping with Brice Marden's career (and his geometric, mathematical, rational Western culture), that his open Zen Buddhist
shape should be a square, not a circle.

What John White has to say of Oriental art is pertinent to Brice
Marden's art, in particular his prints of the late 1970s onwards:

> *In Chinese art the surface emphasis is negative rather than positive. It is in
> close accordance with the calm acceptance, the contemplative natural
> mysticism, which reached its highest flowering in Taoism. The surface is
> left undisturbed. Colours are few, and soft. Ink, and delicate monotone
> washes are the characteristic media. Spiritual and decorative qualities are
> valued high above imitative naturalism, the evocative above the repre-
> sentational... The unmarked silk, or paper, is at once the atmosphere, the
> space, and the inviolate decorative surface.*[7]

In the early 1980s, Brice Marden's art began to change: the
prints and drawings and the paintings began to merge, stylistically
and conceptually. Marden began to use the freedom and openness of his prints in his paintings. He started to paint with a brush
attached to a stick, standing back from the painting, a technique
which recalls James Whistler's arm-length method. Instead of the
dense physicality of oil and wax, Marden took to thinning his
pigments with turpineol. With the new, liquid paint Marden
began treating the paintings in the same way as the drawings and
prints. Dripping, bleeding, scraping and other manifestations of a
looser approach to painting were encouraged. The rigidity and
authority of the rectangle and square and straight lines was
dissolved in a series of webs, crisscrosses, and patterns which
resembled hieroglyphs and Chinese calligraphy. The grid was still
there – one can discern a structure underneath the seemingly
densely interwoven curves and motifs. Verticality was still present:
the intertwined forms were usually vertical, recalling both human

figures and Chinese characters. What Marden explained to the painter Pat Steir about his working method applies to many of his calligraphic drawings, etchings and paintings:

> *I think the closest I get to any sort of meditative state is when I'm drawing. It's about joining up, making relationships, but at the same time letting the drawing itself do the work...Ideally, the drawing is working and I'm working with it.* (in B. Marden, 1991)

This is a typical notion among artists – that the artwork works the artist as well as the other way around. In Zen Buddhist terms, the artist lets the work do itself. It is a descent into the creative, meditative state and a return. A letting-go followed by a reining-in and control.

CHINESE POETRY: THE *ETCHINGS TO REXROTH*
◆

The **Etchings to Rexroth** (1986) series comprises 25 aquatint and sugarlift etchings which directly recall Chinese calligraphy. Brice Marden's **Etchings to Rexroth** use poet Kenneth Rexroth's (1905-82) translations of the Chinese poet Tu Fu (712-770 AD) as a point of departure. This is 'Jade Flower Palace':

> *The stream swirls. The wind moans in*
> *The pines. Grey rats scurry over*
> *Broken tiles. What prince, long ago,*
> *Built this palace, standing in*
> *Ruins beside the cliffs? There are*
> *Green ghost fires in the black rooms.*
> *The shattered pavements are all*

Washed away. Ten thousand organ
Pipes whistle and roar. The storm
Scatters the red autumn leaves.
His dancing girls are yellow dust.
Their painted cheeks have crumbled
Away. His gold chariots
And courtiers are gone. Only
A stone horse is left of his
Glory. I sit on the grass and
Start a poem, but the pathos of
It overcomes me. The future
Slips imperceptibly away.
Who can say what the years will bring?

Poetry is always uppermost in Brice Marden's temperament – his response to Greece, alchemy, the Passion, the Annunciation, and Oriental art is poetic. His art is poetic in the sense of being an intuitive, sensual, non-rational response to subjects. The **Etchings to Rexroth** , therefore, are not precise equivalents of any particular poem or word, but deal in feelings and atmospheres (in fact, Marden said the etchings have more to do with Ezra Pound and his poetic appropriation of Oriental culture than Kenneth Rexroth's Tu Fu translations [P, 146]). Whatever else they are, the etchings are intended to be lyrical, in the way that poetry (usually) must be.

This is 'Winter Dawn' by Tu Fu:

The men and beasts of the zodiac
Have marched over us once more.
Green wine bottles and red lobster shells,
Both emptied, litter the table.
"Should auld acquaintance be forgot?" Each
Sits listening to his own thoughts,
And the sound of cars starting outside.
The birds in the eaves are restless,
Because of the noise and light. Soon now
In the winter dawn I will face
My fortieth year. Borne headlong
Towards the long shadows of sunset

By the headstrong, stubborn moments,
Life whirls past like drunken wildfire.

The **Etchings to Rexroth** explore the delicacy and intricacy of Chinese calligraphy, without resorting to any particular Chinese character or figurative shape. As well as looseness, the **Etchings to Rexroth** are characterized by an energy which is lacking in many of the monochrome and multi-part panels. Simply, the serpentine interweavings of Marden's lines are inevitably full of life. The static and remorseless square/ rectangle is replaced by a kinetic liveliness.

Brice Marden spoke of the importance of responding to nature, and his 'Oriental' works – paintings as well as prints – abound with suggestions of natural forms. Marden spoke of echoing the form of a tree in a drawing, and the way the energy of the natural form of the tree would somehow be expressed in the drawing. Marden described how he would layer drawings on top of each other when in the Far East. He would not use a new sheet of paper for his sketches of trees, rocks, sea shells and mountains, but put today's drawing over yesterday's, hence the multiple layers of his Oriental works. Instead of drawing particular rocks or trees or shells, though, Marden is gathering inspiration from the natural forms, using their energy and essence. The way to read some of the 'Oriental' works, then, is to look below the top layers, at the forms underneath. Some of the **Etchings to Rexroth** depict the forms on their own against the white paper; others, the ones Brice Marden is happier with, are multi-layered, constructed from one shape on top of another.

THE *COLD MOUNTAIN* SERIES
◆

The culmination of Brice Marden's Oriental preoccupations was the **Cold Mountain Series** of paintings and etchings. 'Cold Mountain' (a.k.a Hanshan, 8th-9th centuries) was a Taoist Chinese poet of the Tang dynasty whom Marden discovered in Kenneth Rexroth's translations. A bi-lingual edition of **The Collected Songs of Cold Mountain** [8] enabled Marden to compare the Chinese ideograms with their English translations. This careful study of the relationship between written and visual language, between ideas, sounds, words, pictures, symbols and meanings is wholly in keeping with 1960s Conceptual art (in the explorations between word and image of Lawrence Weiner, Dan Flavin, Bruce Nauman **et al**).

This is one of Cold Mountain's poems:

Since I came to Cold Mountain
How many thousand years have passed?
Accepting my fate I fled to the woods,
To dwell and gaze in freedom.
No one visits the cliffs
Forever hidden by clouds.
Soft grass serves as a mattress,
My quilt is the dark blue sky.
A boulder makes a fine pillow;
Heaven and Earth can crumble and change.

What is instantly striking about the **Cold Mountain** works is their affinity with Jackson Pollock, the painter who presides over so much of contemporary (American) painting (and not only Abstract Expressionism). One sees in Brice Marden's calligraphic paintings the same love of a sinuous, wandering web of lines over a flat, spaceless ground that is the hallmark of Pollock's paintings.

For Marden, Pollock is a postwar artist he prizes above nearly all others. Marden has spoken of the way Pollock, in his mature works, seems to lose himself, to become absorbed in his subject. Brice Marden has spoken affectionately of Pollock's **Scent**:

> Scent *is very peculiar to me, like a real mother earth kind of image. It's very strange. I mean he is kind of lost. Pollock is an incredibly sophisticated and intelligent artist but he sort of loses all that and it just becomes very direct, human expression.* (P, 51)

Something similar occurred in Brice Marden's art from the 1980s onwards. The rigidity and control was gone, to be replaced by a new freedom of expression, an openness which is found in the **Cold Mountain Series** and other paintings, such as **Vine**, **Uxmal**, **The Studio**, the **Couplet** paintings and **Aphrodite**.

The **Cold Mountain Series** are six large paintings (108 by 144 inches) in oil on linen. Five characters, in four couplets, are interwoven over a grid. In the first painting the grid is still visible, but, as usual, Brice Marden progressively layers and complicates the skeins of paint. Although the lines of paint on top of the neutral background are the most spatially deep of Marden's works, they are still extremely flat compared to any of his favourite Old Masters (Rembrandt van Rijn, Francisco de Zurbarán, Édouard Manet and Giovanni Bellini). The **Cold Mountain** paintings are also some of the flattest of contemporary works. Though Marden uses two colors, the lighter paint modulating the darker lines, the **Cold Mountain** works are still very flat, spatially. They recall hugely enlarged depictions of Chinese calligraphic ink on paper. Even the background colors Marden selects for his calligraphic paintings – creams, light browns, pale blues – recall tinted paper or aged, ancient parchment.

The **Cold Mountain Series** are some of the loosest and most 'open' paintings Brice Marden has produced. The **Cold Mountain Series** and related paintings represent a new descent into nature for Marden. Natural forms are embraced – though always modulated by a keen sense of abstraction and language. Marden is not concerned with precise mimesis. He does not hold up a mirror to nature: his **Cold Mountain** and related paintings are at least four or five steps away from nature.

THE PRIMACY OF THE LINE: OTHER CALLIGRAPHIC PAINTINGS
◆

The new works of the mid-1980s onwards are quite different from the 1960s monochromes or the 1970s multi-part panels. When one approaches the later Brice Marden paintings, one is confronted by a quite different object from the 1960s or 1970s panels. The new paintings are in oil on linen, but they are of a different texture, surface, color, light, tone, shape and proportion from the 1970s oil and wax canvas panels. Marden still favoured flattened colors in the calligraphic paintings: the backgrounds are in 'neutral' colors, such as grey (**The Studio**), green-grey (**Kalo Keri**), grey-pink (**Presentation**), muted yellow (**Aphrodite**) and pale blue (**Uxmal**). The scale of the calligraphic paintings is of a similar order to the mid-1970s canvases: 96 inches is a typical height. Many of the paintings are not, however, vertical in format. Paintings such as **Vine, Virgins** and **Aphrodite** are, like the **Cold**

Mountain paintings, horizontal rectangles. Every interior calligraphic motif, though, is in a vertical format, and repeated, with variations, across the horizontal expanse of the painting. Each Pollockian serpentine mark is in a different color: in **Virgins** (1991-3, private collection), there are faint violet, sepia and sand-hued lines of paint. In **Uxmal** (1991-3, private collection), turquoise, green, khaki and brown lines of oil are drawn on top of a violet-blue background. The colors of the calligraphic paintings are always related to the single, light color of the background. The use of different colors for each curving line makes each motif clearer, extending Marden's technique of adding gouache to his ink calligraphic drawings.

Presentation (1990-2, private collection) is unusual amongst Brice Marden's calligraphic paintings, for it employs a wide-ish range of colors, from white, to yellow, red and black, recalling Marden's use of brilliant color in the mid-1970s works (such as **For Hera,** the **Moon** series and the **Red, Yellow, Blue** series).

Regarding Brice Marden's calligraphic paintings, one is struck by formal aspects similar to Jackson Pollock's paintings: complexity of interweaving lines; the primacy of line and geometry over color; spatial flatness; semi-organic/ natural forms; allusive/ metaphoric shapes; a single tone; unity of form, and so on. (Marden consciously evoked organic forms in his 'calligraphic' works, such as the double helix of DNA, and one of his passions, sea shells, in particular the family of sea shells called volutes, which Marden has collected).

The **Shell Drawings** in ink on paper (1985-87, collection: the artist) start out relatively simple, as so often in Brice Marden's series of works, and gradually become complex. The motifs seem to evoke the volute shell form in the first drawings, but in the later **Shell Drawings** the marks lose their isolated identities, and merge into the now-familiar Marden vertical glyphs.

Later print and drawings series which echoed Chinese calligraphy include **The Virgins, Cyprian Album, Five Woodland Poems, Han Shan Exit 1-6, Tu Fu Dog** and **Grace Notes.** In the etchings and drawings of the 1990s, Brice Marden's preoccupations with the painters known as the Old Masters was still strong. A series of etchings and aquatints of 1992-3 was entitled **After Botticelli**.

THE RETURN OF THE FIGURE: FIGURATIVE WORKS
◆

Of course, Brice Marden's post-1980 prints and paintings are not 'authentically' Oriental. They are remain Western art objects, products of a particular sort of socio-political environment. They are art objects which exist in the top of the range, professional, international art world, of expensive New York lofts and galleries, large and grandiose retrospectives at the Guggenheim, Tate and Stedelijk museums. In the midst of Marden's calligraphic works, for example, the figure is very much in evidence. Marden's move towards the East has not expunged figuration and representation. Instead of the paintings becoming more and more 'empty' and less and less representational, they are in fact progressively figurative and representational. Nature and the figure have always been present in Marden's art, in the **Back Series** and the **Sea Paintings,** for example. The paintings and etchings of the late 1980s and early 1990s were full of the usual allusions to nature, and in particular, to Greece: 'Cyprian Album', 'Aphrodite'.

In **The Virgins** series of drawings in ink on T.H. Saunders paper (1991-3, private collection), the figures become increasingly complex and overlayered, until, in **The Virgins 8**, they are covered by a multiplicity of lines. In the later stages of **The Virgins**, Brice Marden adds lines of pale blue gouache over his calligraphic forms, which further modulate the figures. Series of drawings, such as the **Cyprian Album** of 1992-3 (private collection) and **Five Woodland Poems** (1992-3), reprise Marden's technique of beginning with an isolated motif and building up layers of connected motifs on top of it.

The human figure in Brice Marden's 1980s and 1990s work becomes not abstracted so severely, as in the **Back Series** or the **Annunciation Series**. Instead, the figure steps forward and becomes easily discernible in amongst the loose, relaxed squiggles. There are a number of figurative drawings in ink on paper in which the human figure is described with open black curves. Marden does not make every aspect of the figure explicit. Nor does he draw the face, that final indication of intimacy and humanity. Instead, in **The Virgins** series, in **Untitled Figure Drawing 2** and **Figure,** the figure is a faceless, universal type, which recalls Greek statuary, or, going back further, the 'stone Venuses', the squat, callipygous palæolithic figurines. These female figures, with the breasts and hips and legs clearly but also shakily marked, express a return to the figure for Marden after years of radical Postminimal abstraction.

CHAPTER *10*

Brice Marden and Other Painters

A PAINTER who shares much in common with Brice Marden is Robert Ryman (b. 1930). Like Marden, Ryman explored the relation between color and the sensuality of surfaces in his really sumptuous white squares. Ad Reinhardt also painted rigorously monochrome paintings, his black-on-black squares (though Robert Rauschenberg had painted all-black paintings before Reinhardt). Jasper Johns' use of grey, and Ad Reinhardt's and Robert Rauschenberg's use of black, influenced the 1960s monochrome painters, such as Brice Marden, Frank Stella and Ryman.[1] Ryman delved into the mysticality of white-on-white, as Kasimir Malevich had done. Paintings of Ryman's such as **Untitled,** a small painting by contemporary standards (53.5 inches square), or the very small **Untitled** of 1961 (12 inches square), displayed a sense of the tactile to rival Jasper Johns. Ryman's art, like Marden's, was founded on the sensuality of paint, of surfaces, of the eroticism of texture, and how sensuality related to color and form.[2] We come back to this again and again in art criticism, this sensualism of surface. As Lynda Nead writes of Kenneth Clark: 'Clark reads brush marks and lines as though they are part of a symbolic language of sensual impulses, telling traces of sexual desire.'[3]

By limiting himself to white, Robert Ryman, like Brice Marden, freed himself up for an exploration of different formal aspects. In Ryman's case, the formal exploration included moving through a range of media, for Ryman painted in white on many kinds of material: canvas, linen, cotton, wood, paper, steel, copper, aluminium, mylar, fibreglass, Plexiglas and cardboard. He painted with different sorts of media: oil, baked enamel, paper, vinyl acetate emulsion, etc. As Ryman said, typically of so many contemporary artists:

> There is never a question of what to paint, but only how to paint (in D. Wheeler, 207).

There are a host of Post-Painterly Abstract artists who make the sensuality of surface primary in their works: Jean Dubuffet and Antoni Tapiès love to crowd their surfaces with mixtures of materials; Anselm Keifer sticks bits of straw onto his oil paintings. There are any number of contemporary painters for whom touch and surface are crucial: such as Julian Schnabel, Thérèse Oulton, Gillian Ayres and Jennifer Bartlett. Sean Scully's painterly surfaces recall Marden's oil and wax treatments, as do those of Howard Hodgkin; Scully's formal innovations with a small separate square canvas pushed into a larger set of panels bolted together also recalls Marden's multi-part paintings.

☆

Many contemporary painters are self-consciously 'messy' – think of John Walker, Michael Porter, Amat, K.H. Hödicke, Enzo Cucchi and Francis Bacon. Freudians have things to say about artists who are deliberately 'messy'. Aesthetically, the explosion into chaos and mess helps to renew the connection with the eroticism of texture, with the sexuality of texture and the sensuality of surface, which has always been a large part of art. Think of Italian Renaissance painting, with all the punched and embossed gold, which provides the spaceless, divine background to Jesus and the Virgin in so many altarpieces and panels. Contemporary painting counters the fake purity and tidiness in advertizing and digital art by loading its canvases with thick paint and impasto marks, and with all manner of materials, from plants to metal to wood to paper. Computers and screens can't reproduce these sensual surfaces.

Other painters who have affinities with Brice Marden include Gerhard Richter (b. 1932), who is renowned as an influential figurative and abstract painter, a painter of representations such as the softly smeared **Annunciations After Titian** (1973), a series of metapaintings, paintings about paintings, which explored Renaissance art in terms of postmodernism. Richter is not, like Marden, wholly (or nearly wholly) abstract. 1980s paintings by Richter such as **Untitled (531-4)** and **Group of Trees (628-1)**, are near-abstract pieces, consisting of thick brushstrokes, in the Willem de Kooning or Howard Hodgkin manner. The more abstract painting, **Untitled**, still retains notions of representation: it has a 'background' space to the foreground shapes which is a light blue, something like the smooth, clear skies of Yves Tanguy's dreamscapes.

There are many painters who traverse the boundaries between abstraction and figuration, who make blurred shapes and patterns on canvas which hint at representation, while remaining inexplicable and 'abstract': Andreas Schulze, Helmut Middendorf, Helmut Federle, Julian Schnabel, Anselm Keifer, Thérèse Oulton, Albert Oehlen, Mimmo Paladino and Herbert Brandl. The painters, sometimes called Neo-Expressionists or **Neue Wilde**, make powerful gestures which are also deliberately vague, ambivalent and non-didactic. Their paintings are very strident, in the 'expressionist' style, with much fierce, energetic application of paint. But the shapes, patterns, forms and tones suggest figuration (figures, bits of architecture, shadows), while also simply being brushstrokes. Per Kirkeby's **Winter VI** is a tall canvas with tones ranging from white to black, yet the forms, which hint at architectonics, remain abstract. Herbert Brandl's **Untitled** is an Expressionist mass of dark reds and blacks, a swirl of paint which suggests a storm in the manner of J.M.W. Turner's paintings of the Alps. This is a simplistic, Romantic reading of a painting which is nothing to do with a Turnerian storm, even though, at a physical level, in terms of the physical look of paint on canvas, there is a similarity between Turner's and Brandl's technique.

Helmut Middendorf's **Aeroplane Dream** (1982) has a more descriptive title than the ubiquitous **Untitled**, the most popular title in contemporary art. The dark black plane, though, is barely visible in the deep blue of the sky. The painting is more about the application of paint in luscious colors than about an aeroplane, although the dream-like quality is affirmed in the use of dark blues. Helmut Federle's **Three Shapes, Two Crossed**, reworks Ad Reinhardt's reductive Minimal painting, with its dark blue crosses on dark green. The religious connotations are close to Marden's own paintings, and the cross motif recalls Marden's **Thira**. John Armleder's **Untitled** is very Marden-like: a horizontal painting of two colors: flat yellow/ ochre and beige, and nothing else. But it has a round wooden table in front of it, which radically alters the abstract painting hanging behind it.

Brice Marden's influence continues to be seen in contemporary painters, and his works have remained some of the most enduring and valuable productions of the Minimal and 1970s period. Marden's art, however, transcends its origins in Minimalism, and takes its place among the richest artworks of the contemporary era.

ILLUSTRATIONS

Featuring artists and art which have influenced Brice Marden.

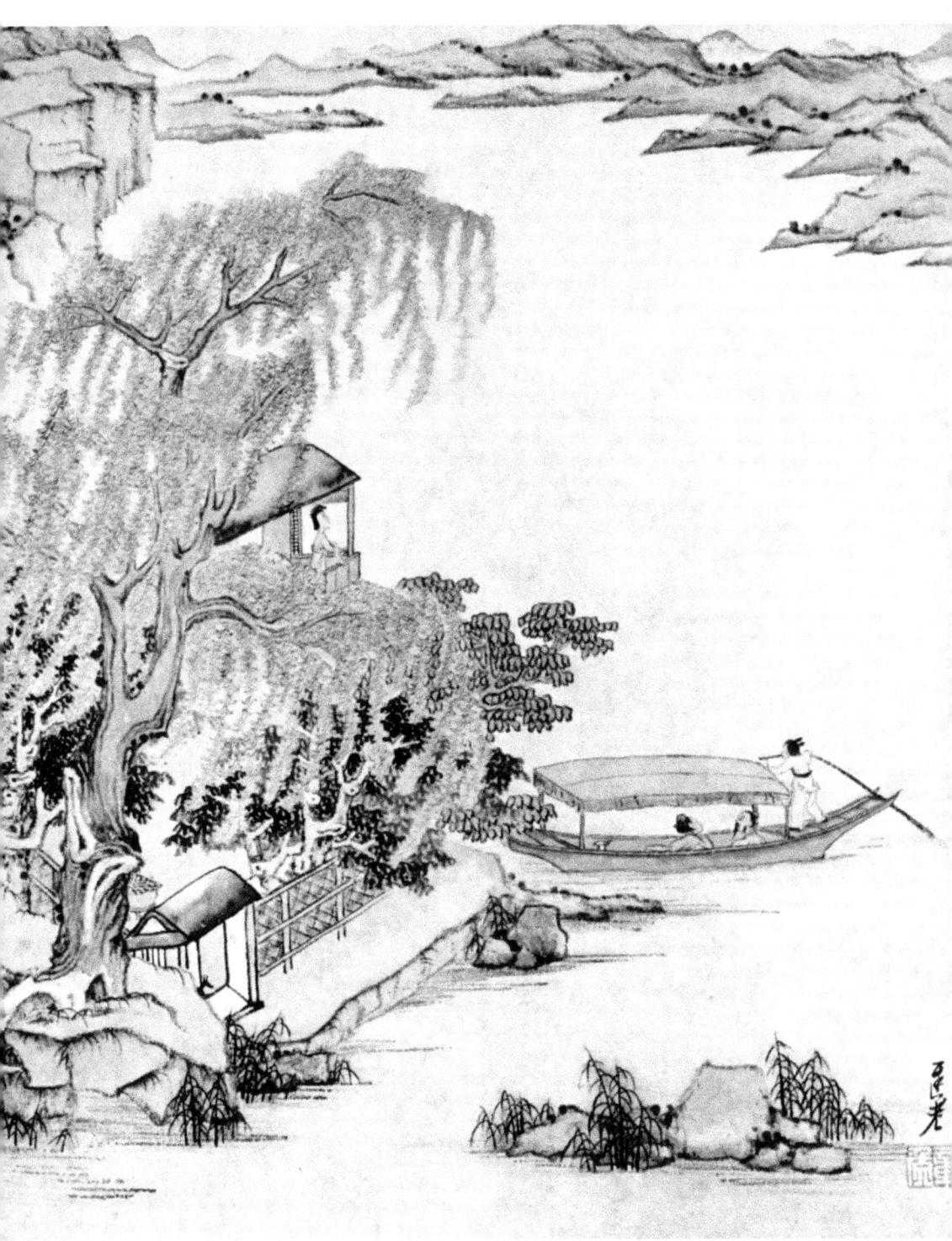

Chinese Landscape, Ming Dynasty, 1630-1650

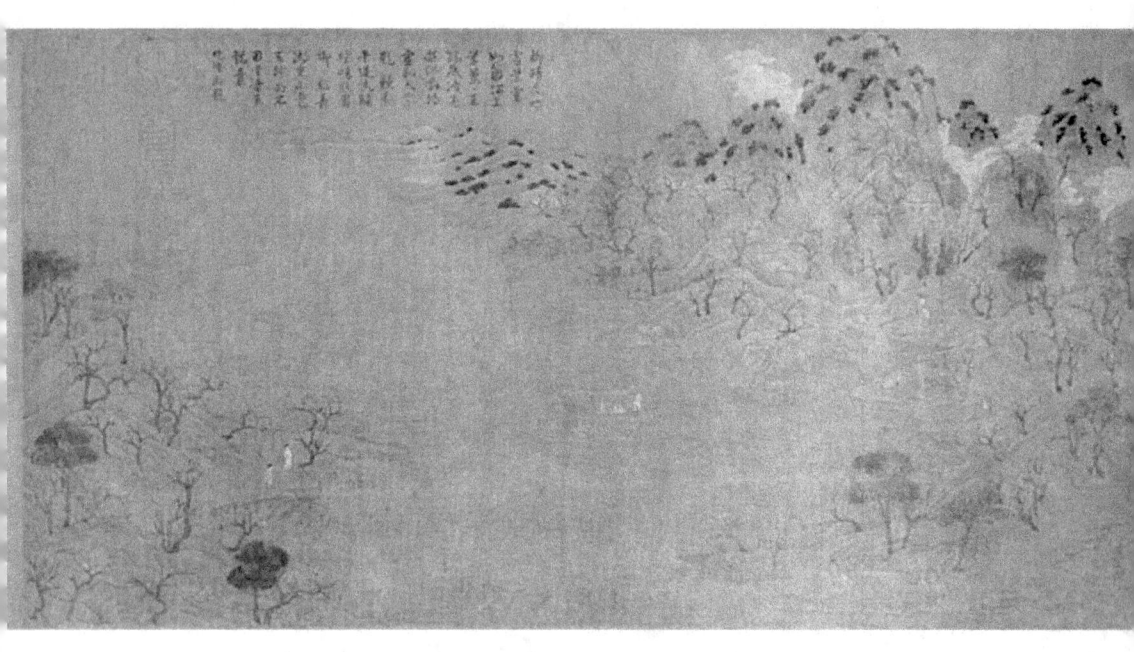

Zhan Ziqia, Stroll About In Spring, c. 600, Sui Dynasty

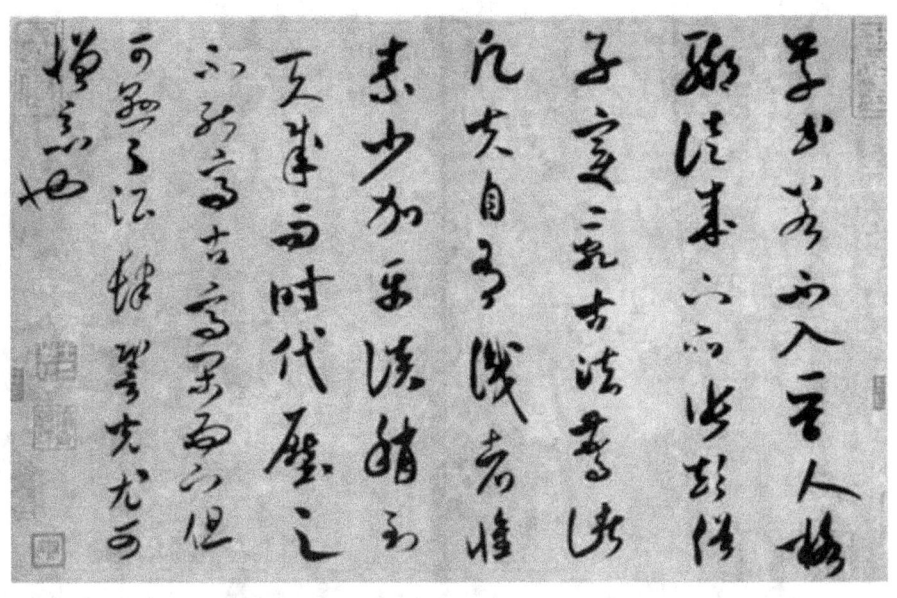

Chinese calligraphy written by poet Mi Fu (1051-1108), Song Dynasty

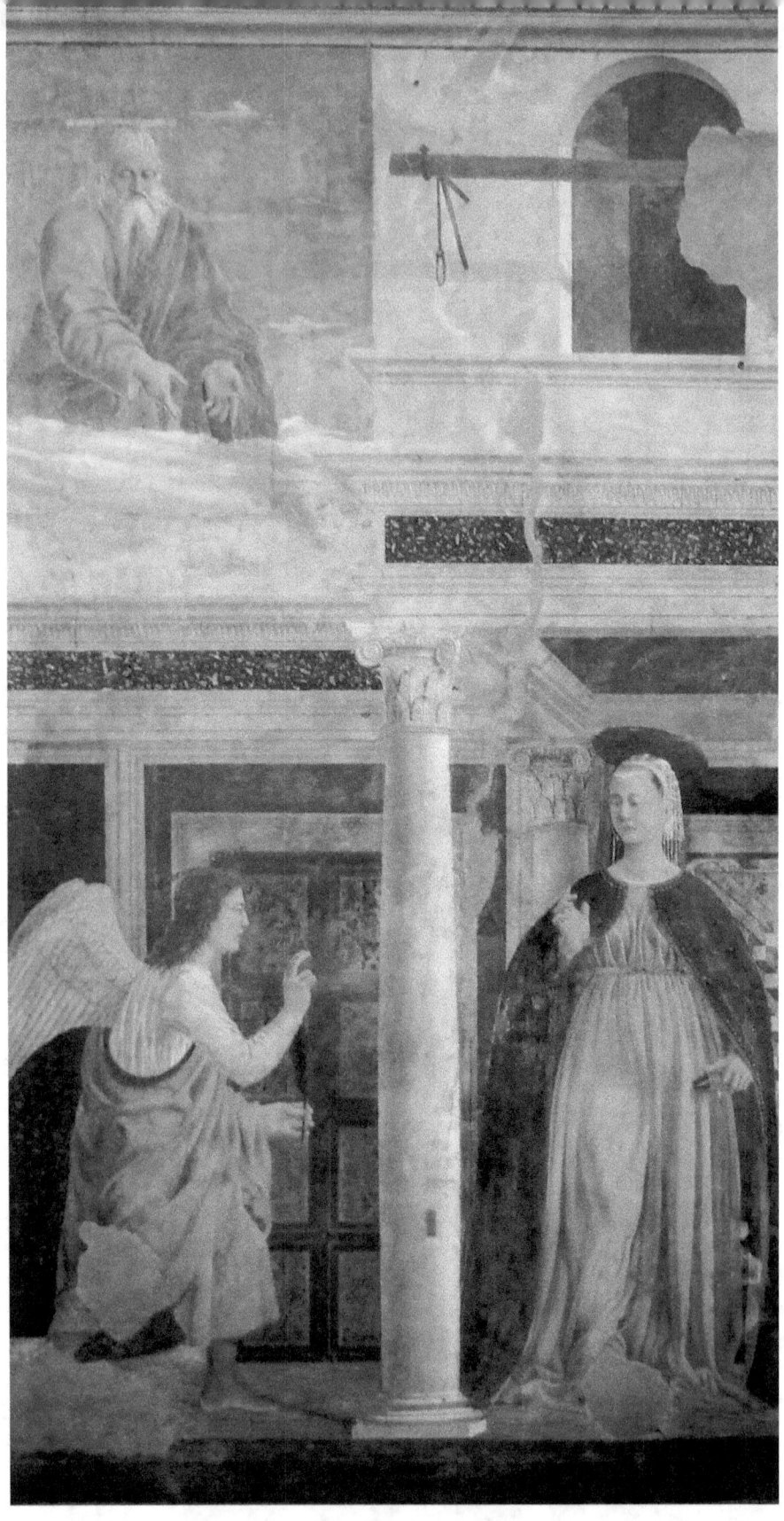

Piero, The Annunciation, Arezzo

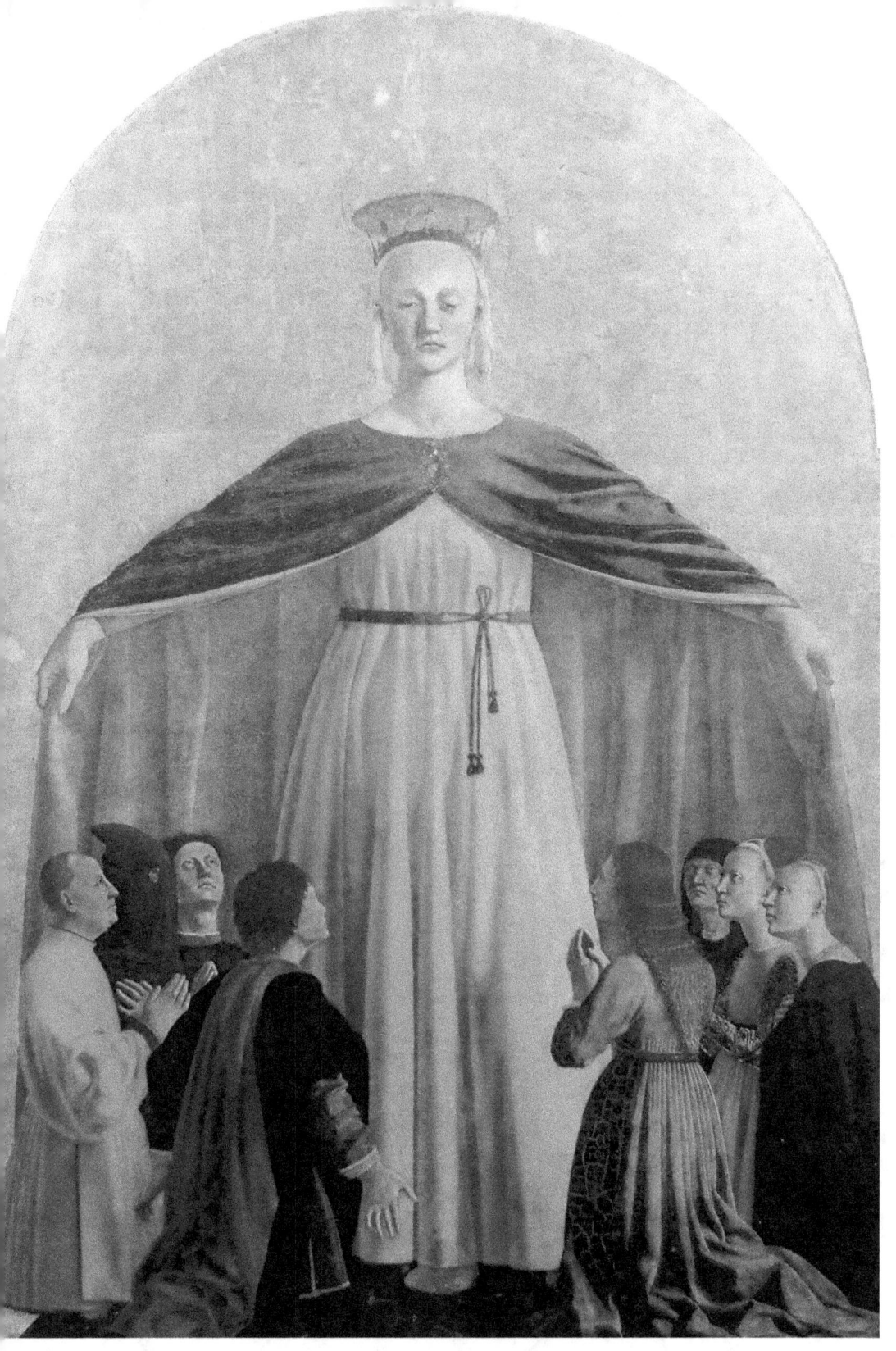

Piero, Madonna della Misericordia, Sanepulchro

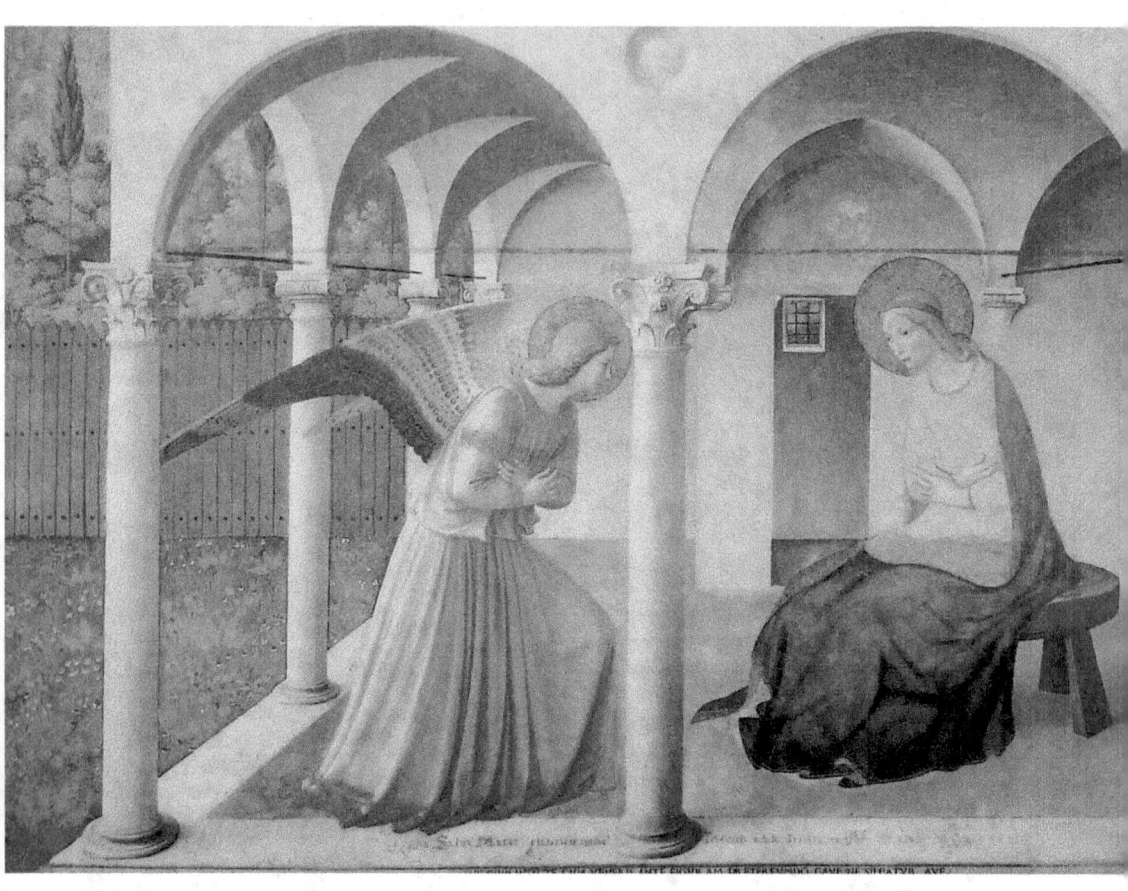

Fra Angelico, The Annunciation, San Marco, Florence

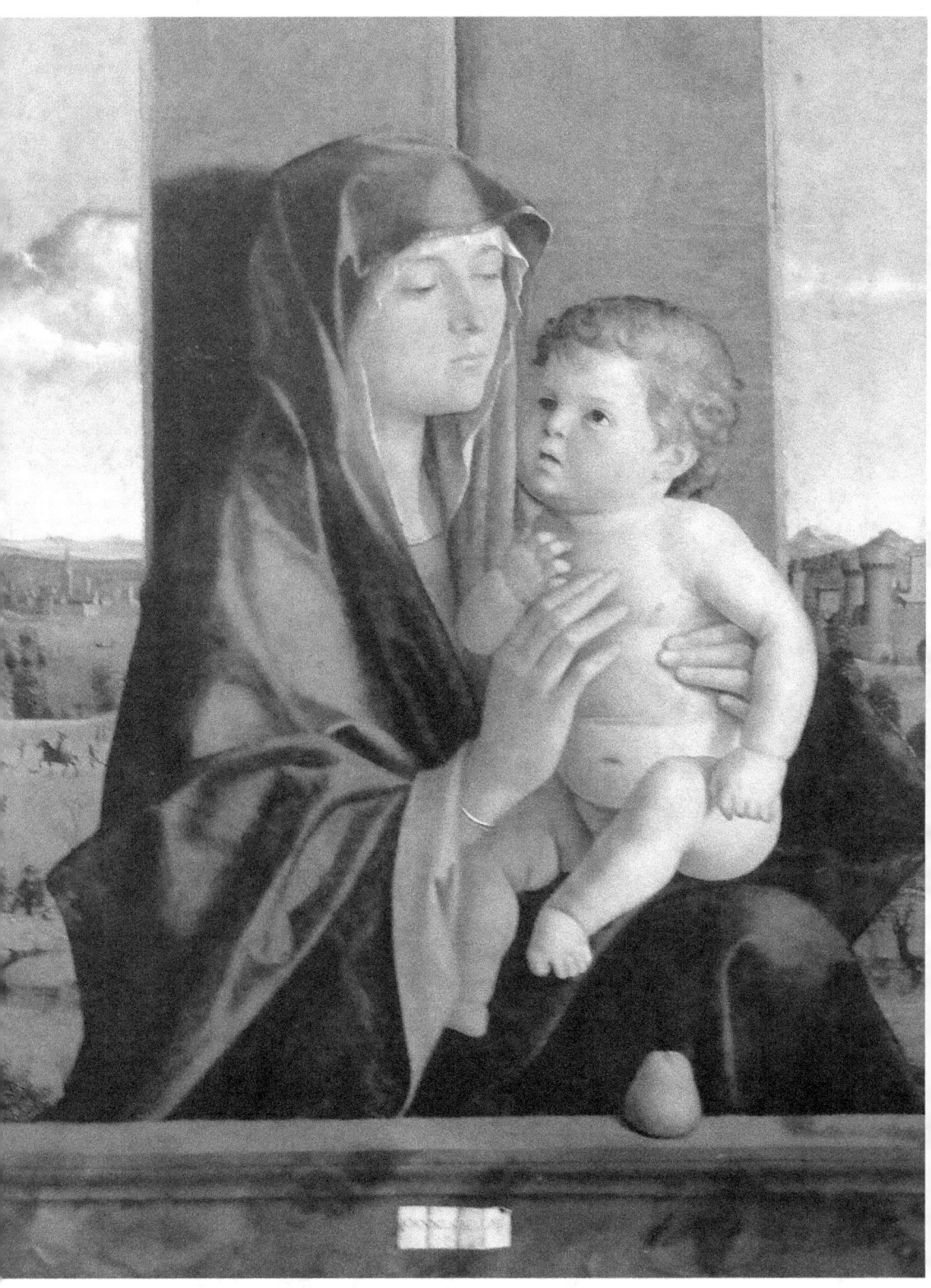

Giovanni Bellini, The Virgin and Child, Bergamo

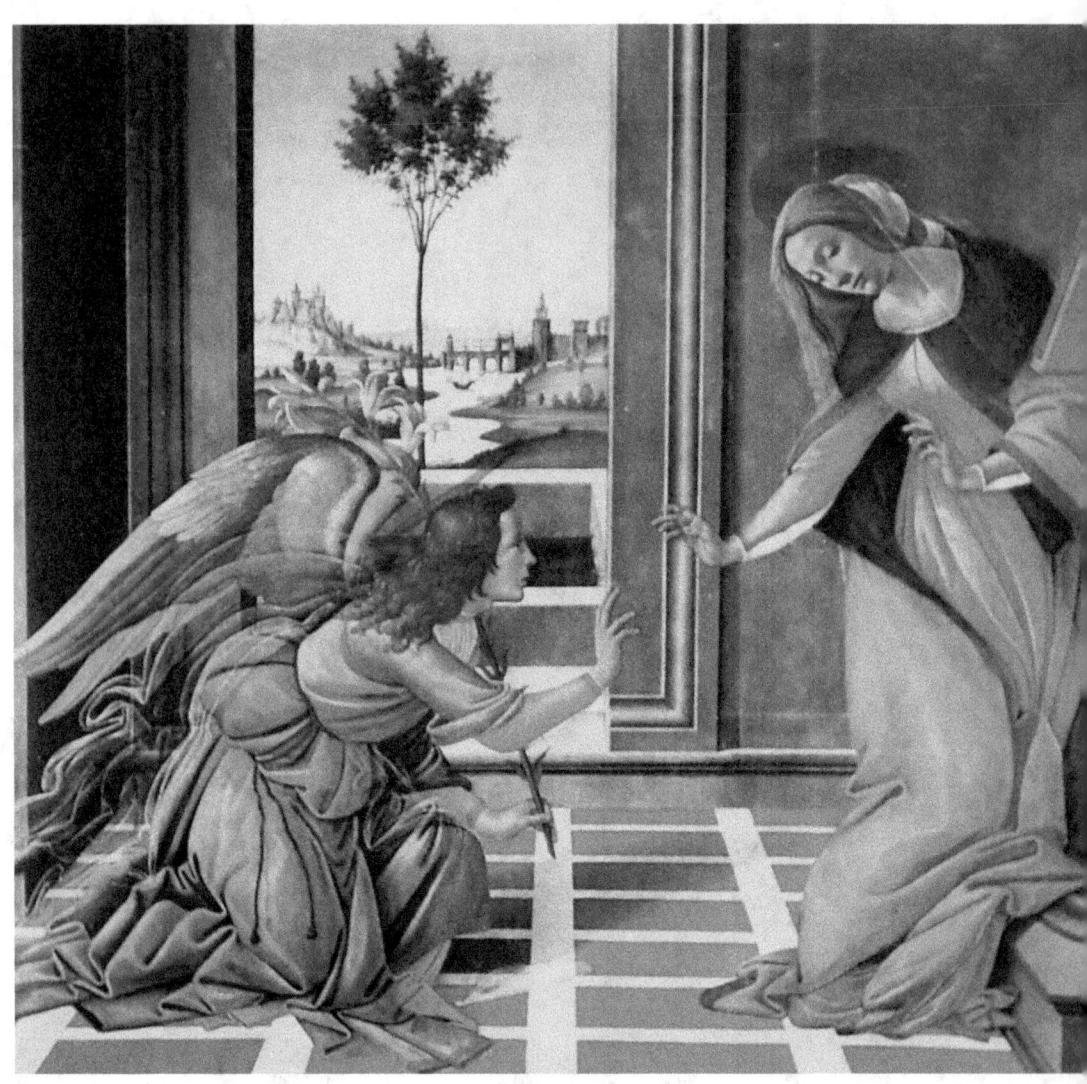

Sandro Botticelli, The Annunciation, Uffizi Gallery, Florence

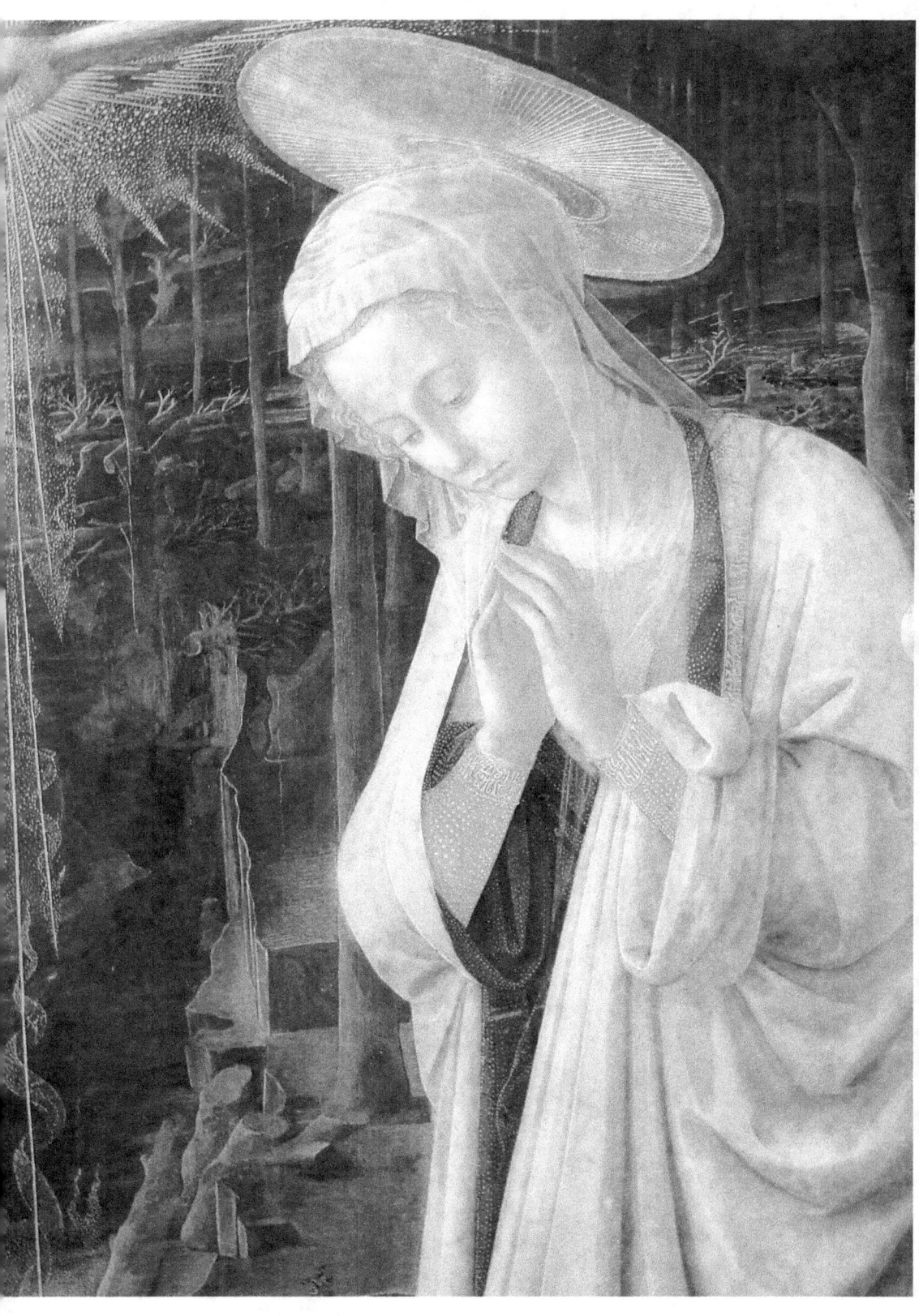

Fra Filippo Lippi, The Adoration of the Virgin, Berlin, detail

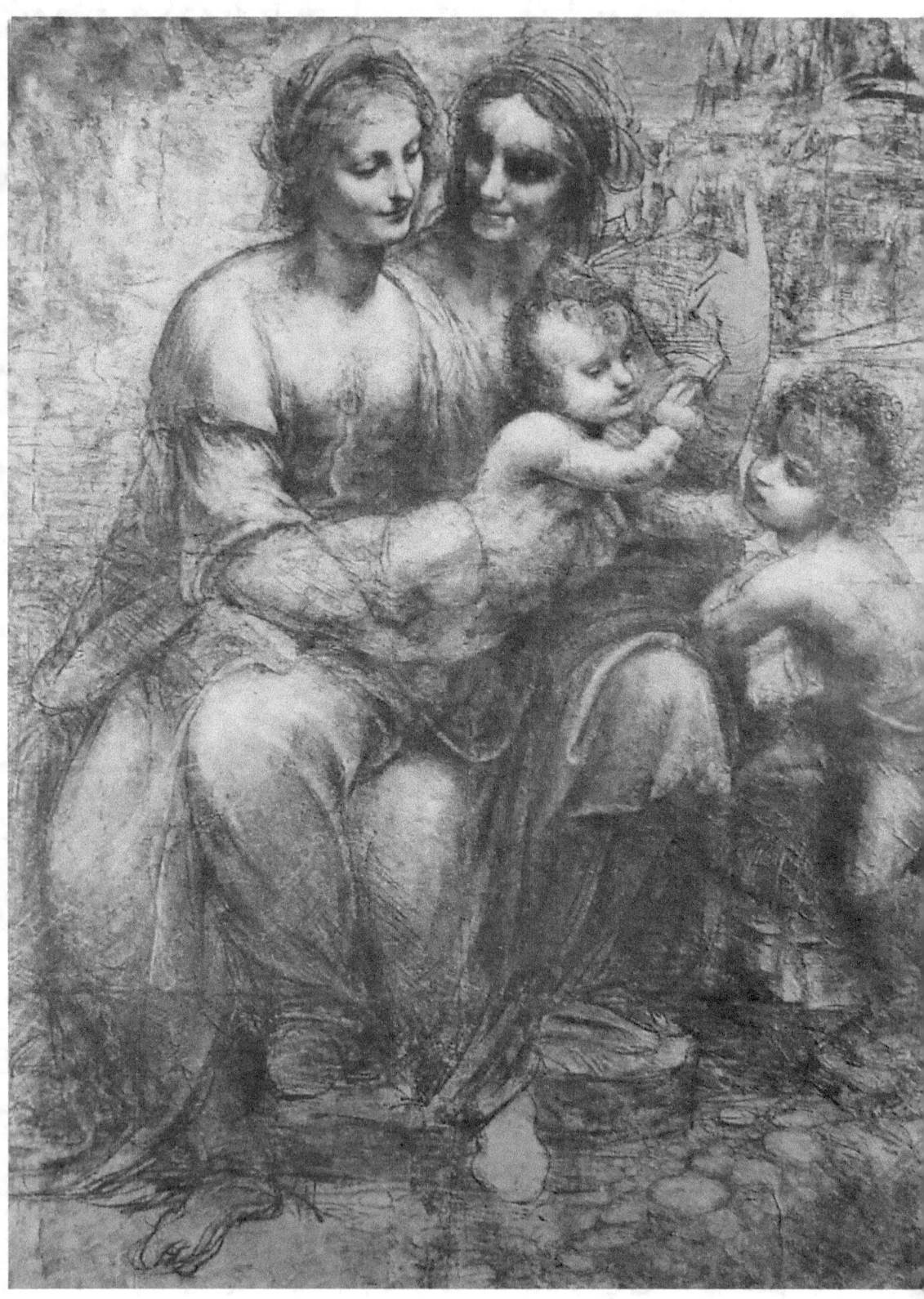

Leonardo, The Virgin and Child With St Anne, National Gallery, London

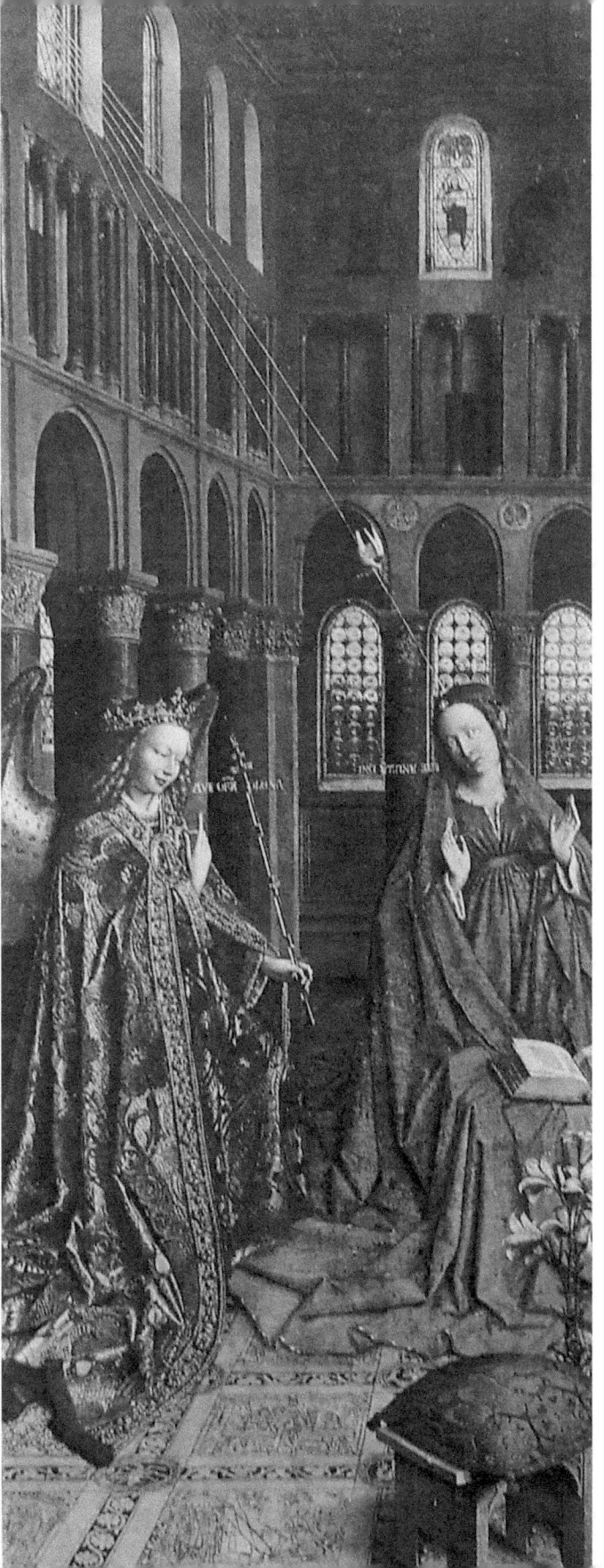

Jan van Eyck,
The Annuncia-
tion, National
Gallery of Art,
Washington, DC

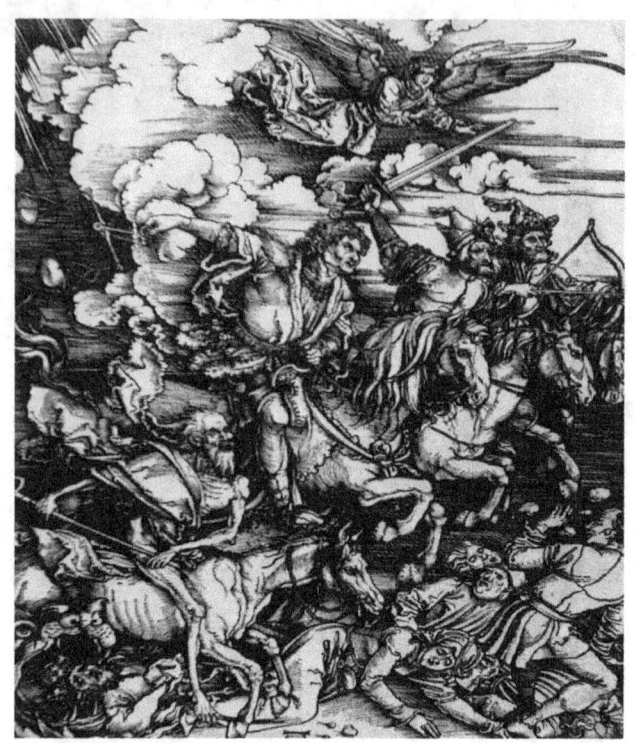

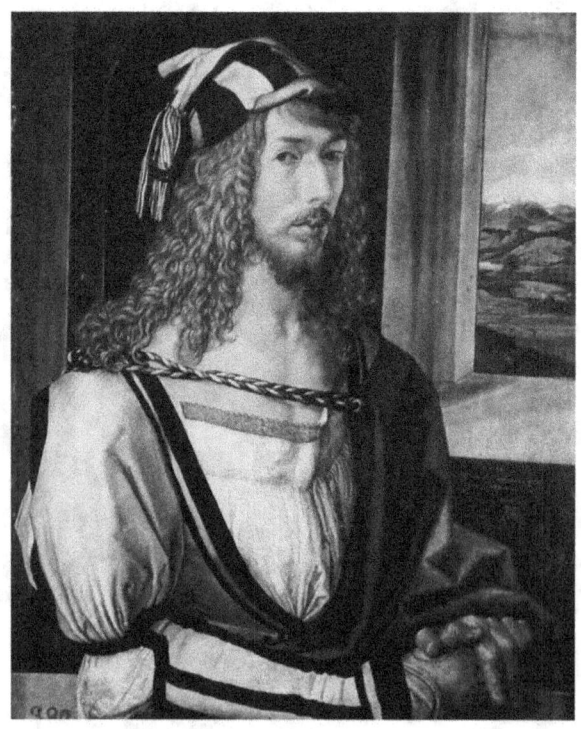

Albrecht Dürer

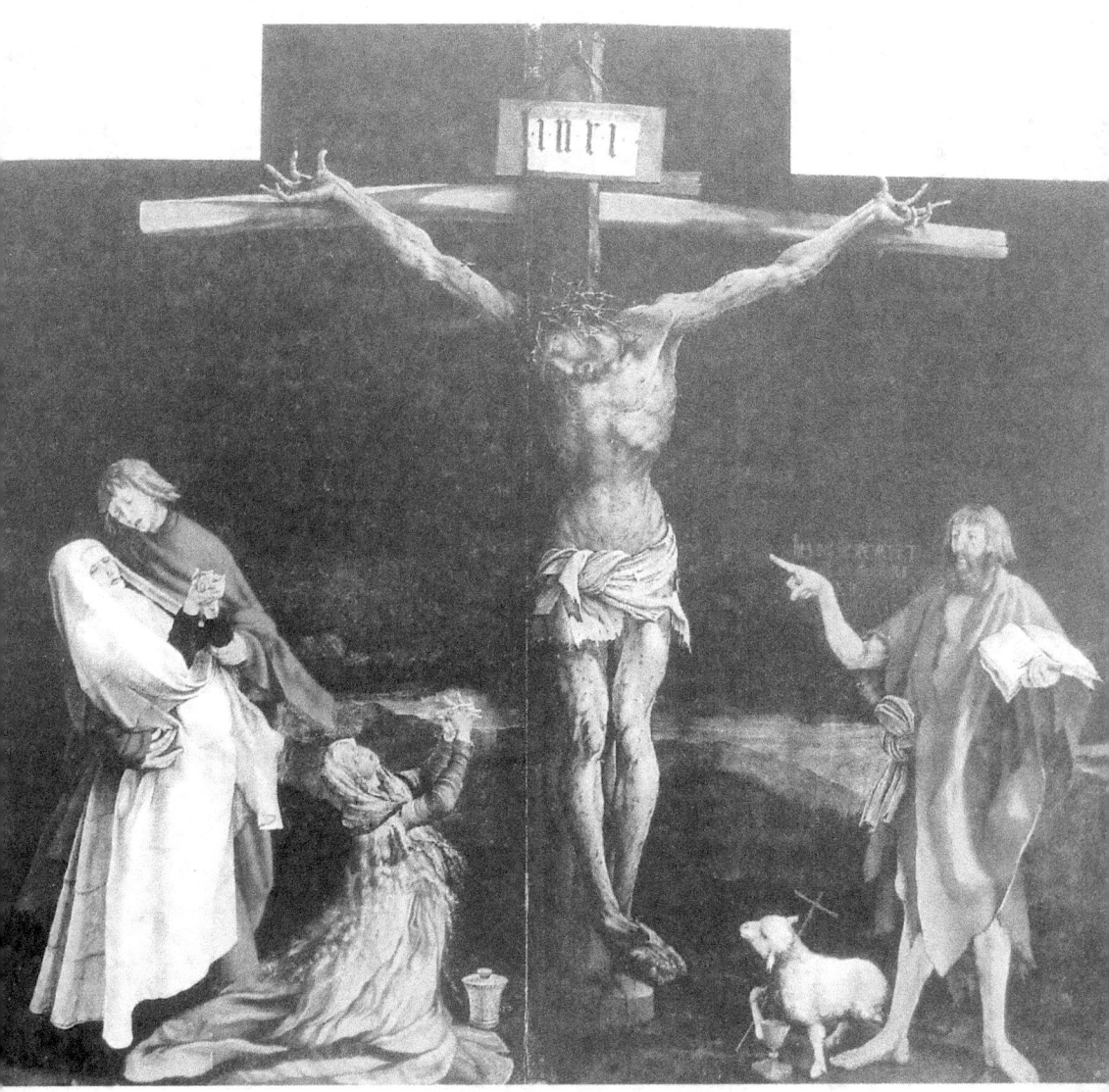

Matthias Grünewald, Crucifixion, Isenheim Altarpiece

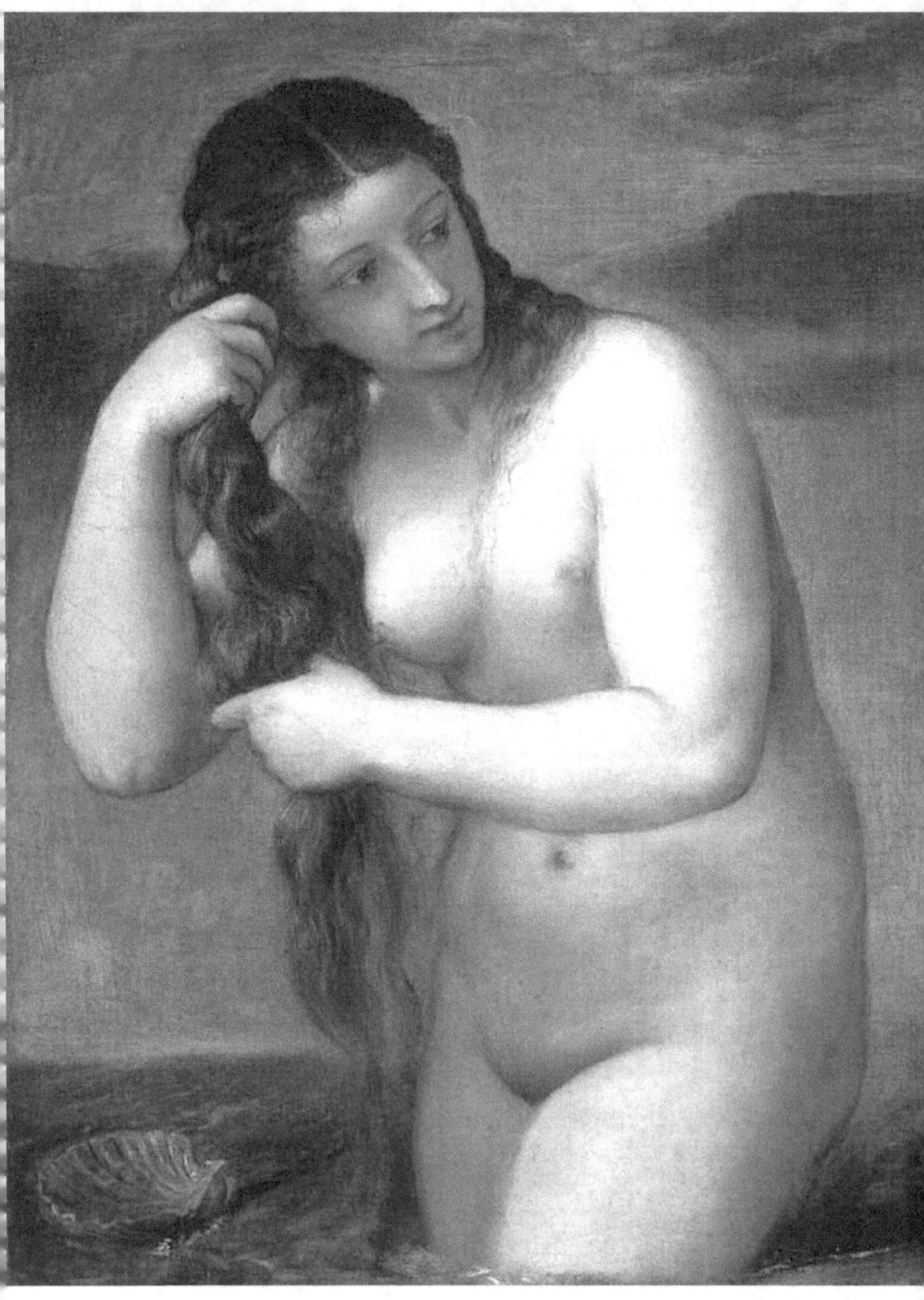

Titian, Venus Rising From the Sea, 1520, Scotland

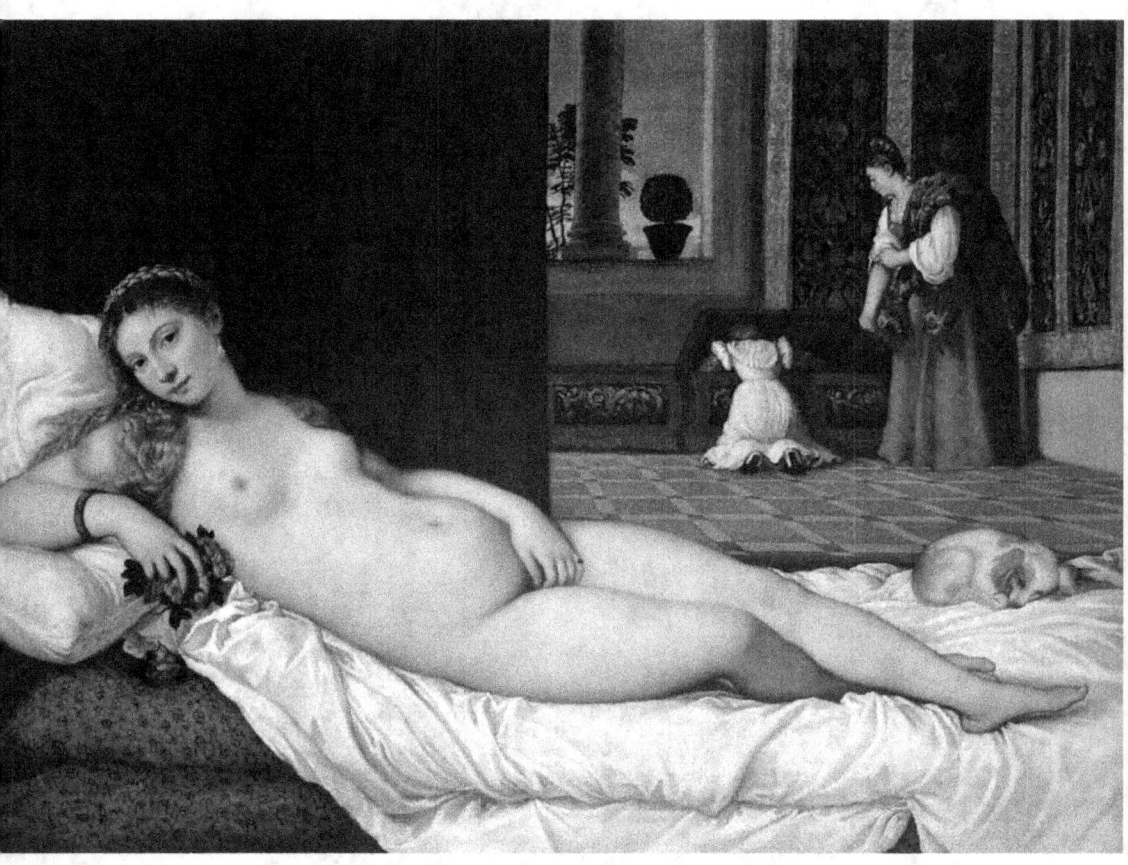

Titian, The Venus of Urbino, 1538, Uffizi, Florence

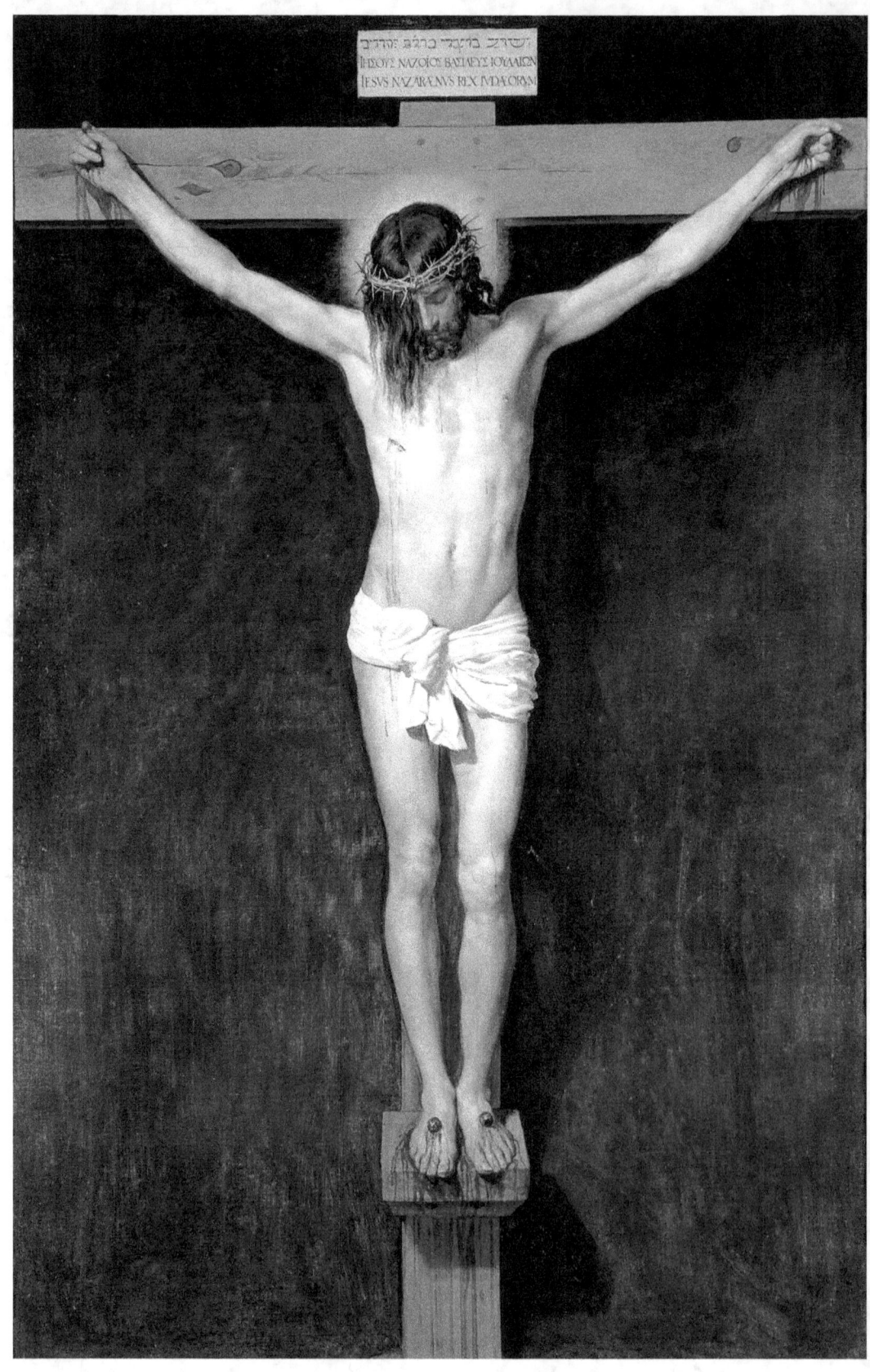

Diego Velásquez, Christ Crucified, 1632, Prado, Madrid

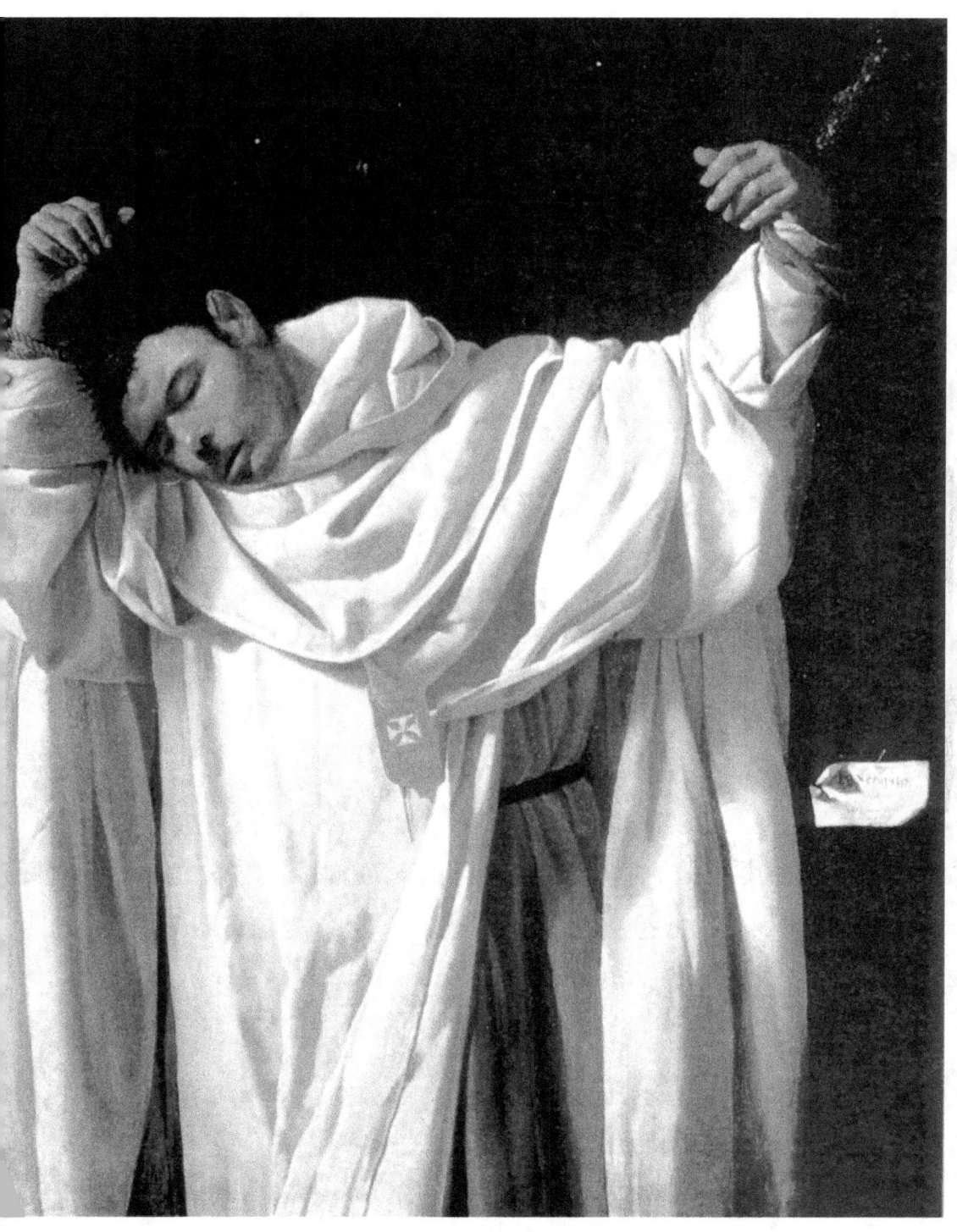

Francisco de Zurbarán, St Serapion, 1628, Hartford, Connecticut

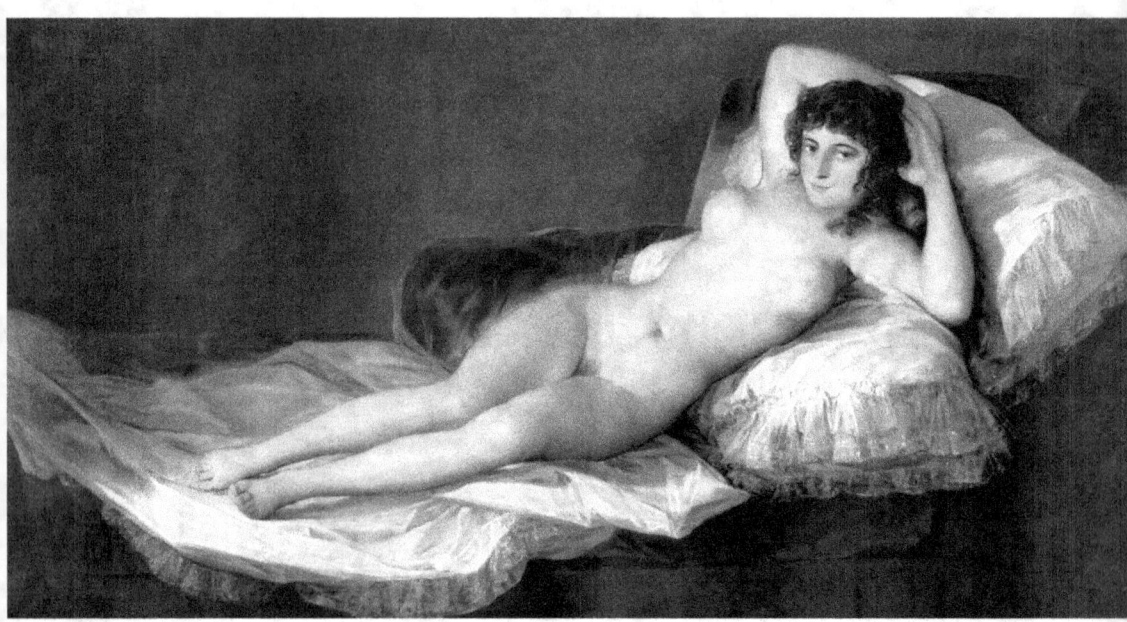

Francisco de Goya, Naked Maja, c. 1801, Prado, Madrid

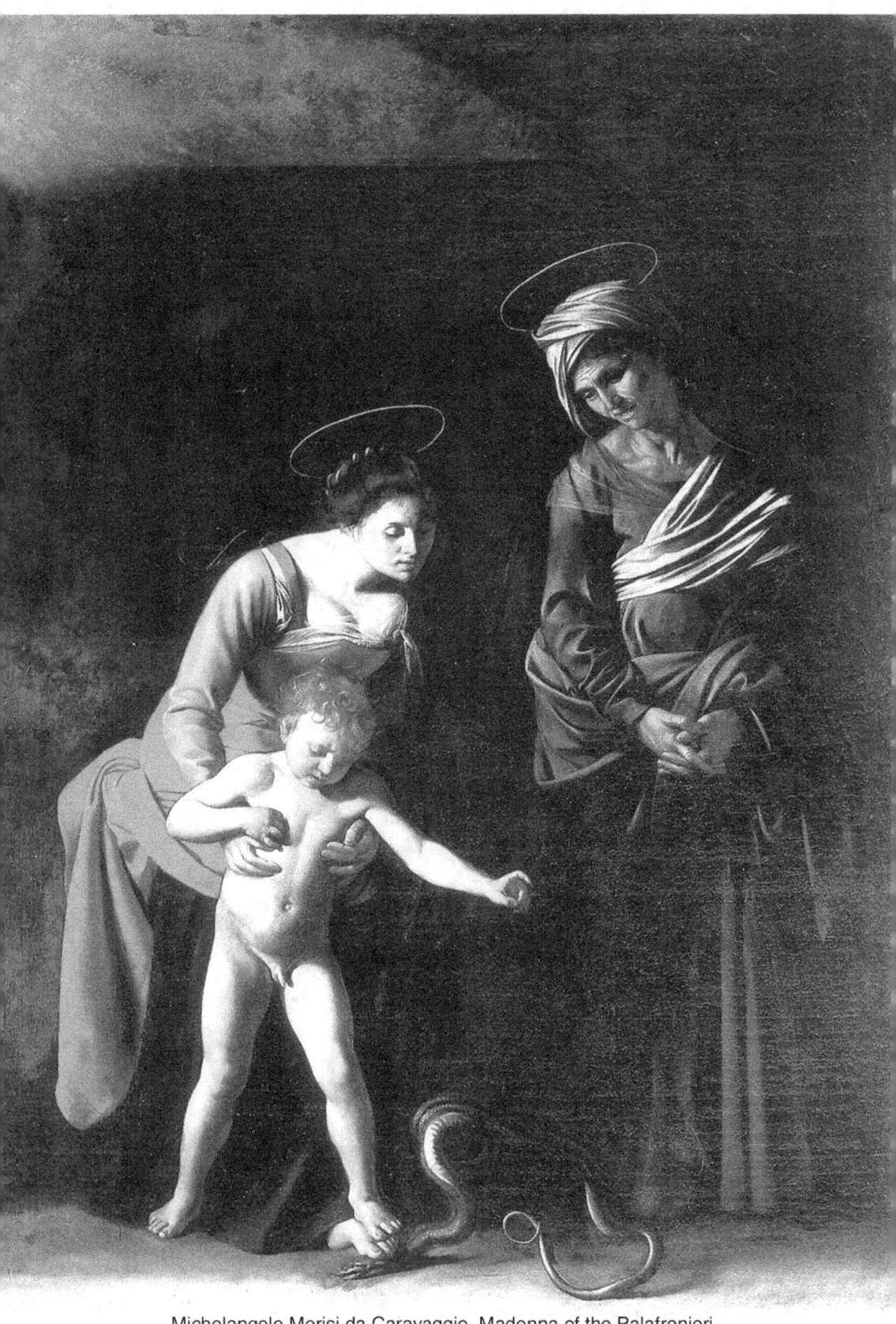

Michelangelo Merisi da Caravaggio, Madonna of the Palafrenieri,
1605-06, Galleria Borghese, Rome

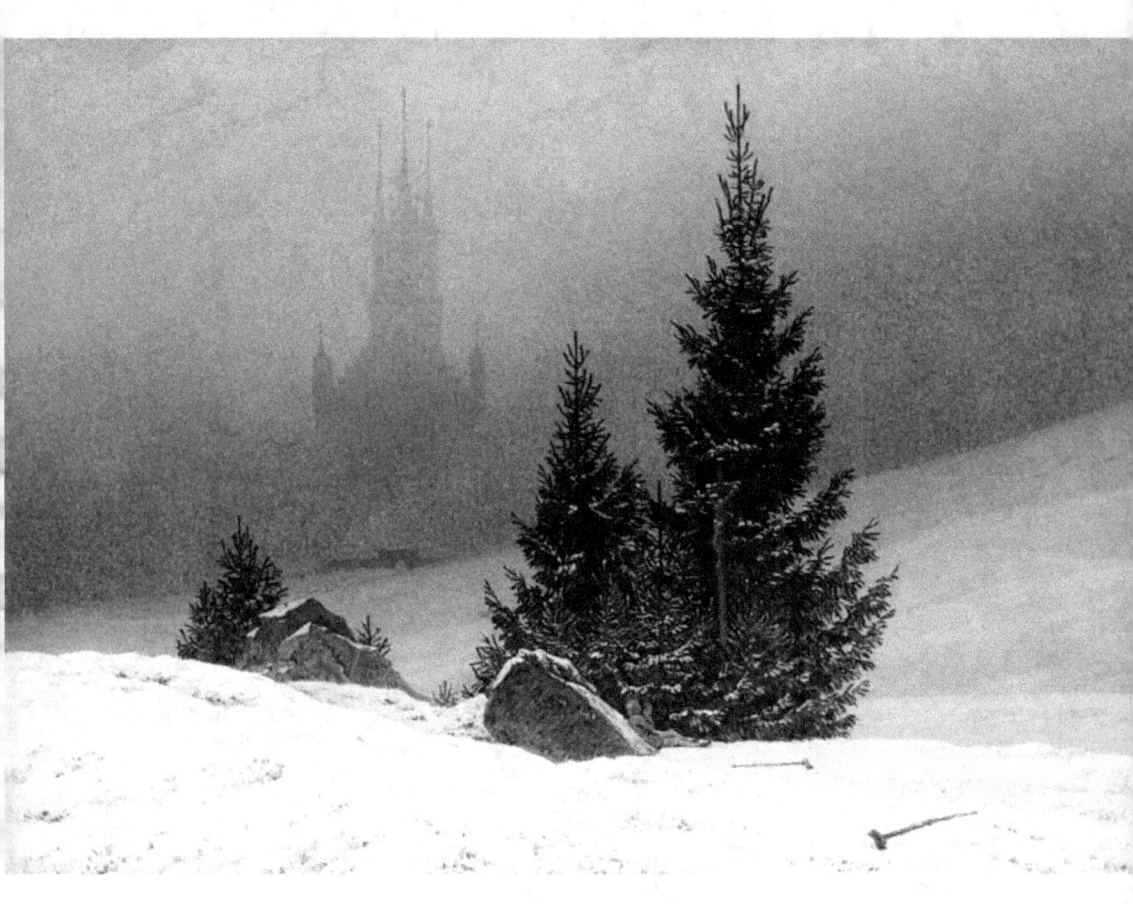

Casper David Friedrich, Winter Landscape, 1811, National Gallery, London

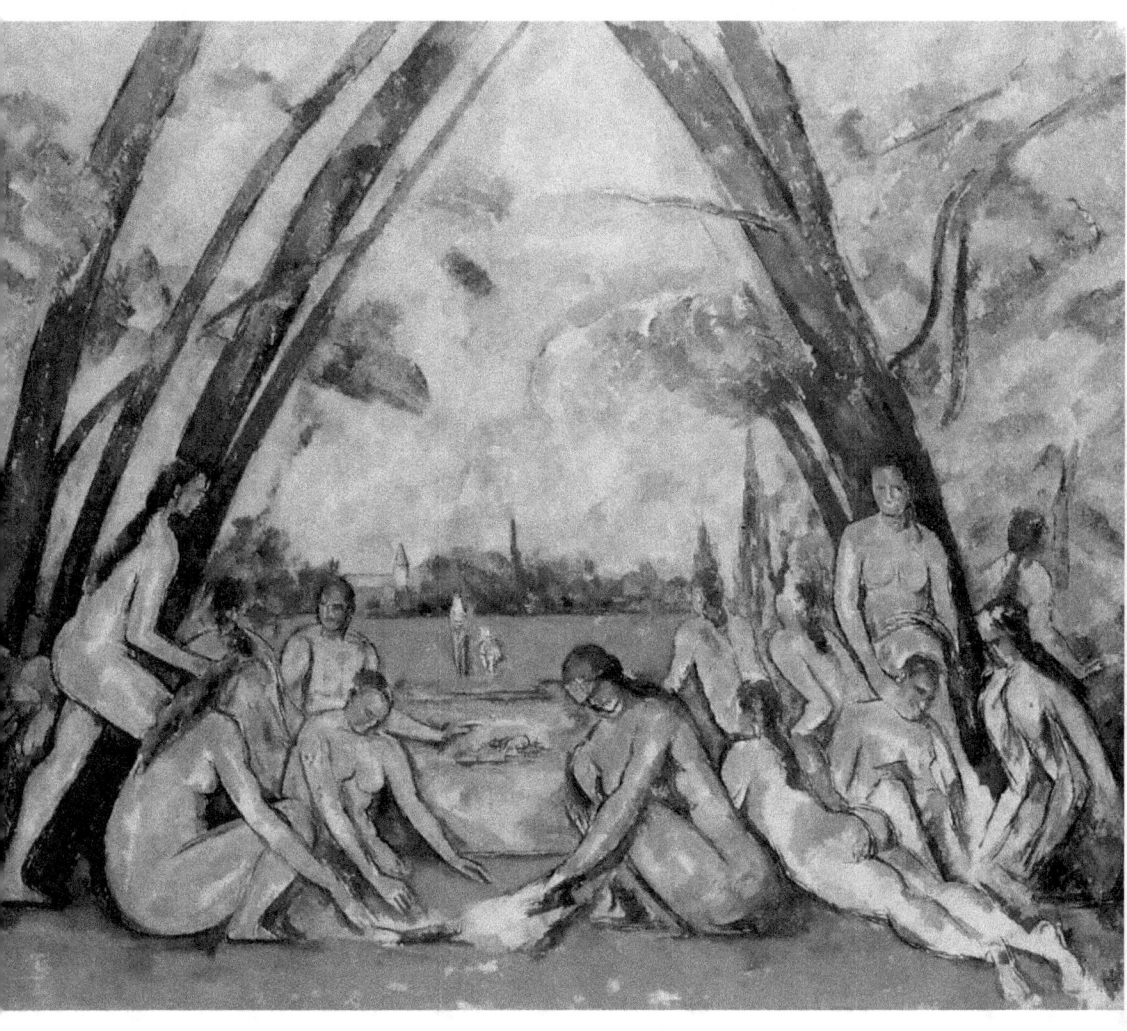

Paul Cézanne, Large Bathers, 1906,
Philadelphia Museum of Art

Kasimir Malevich, Black Painting, St Petersburg

From Robert Fludd's
Utriusque Cosmi maioris salicet et minoris metaphysica

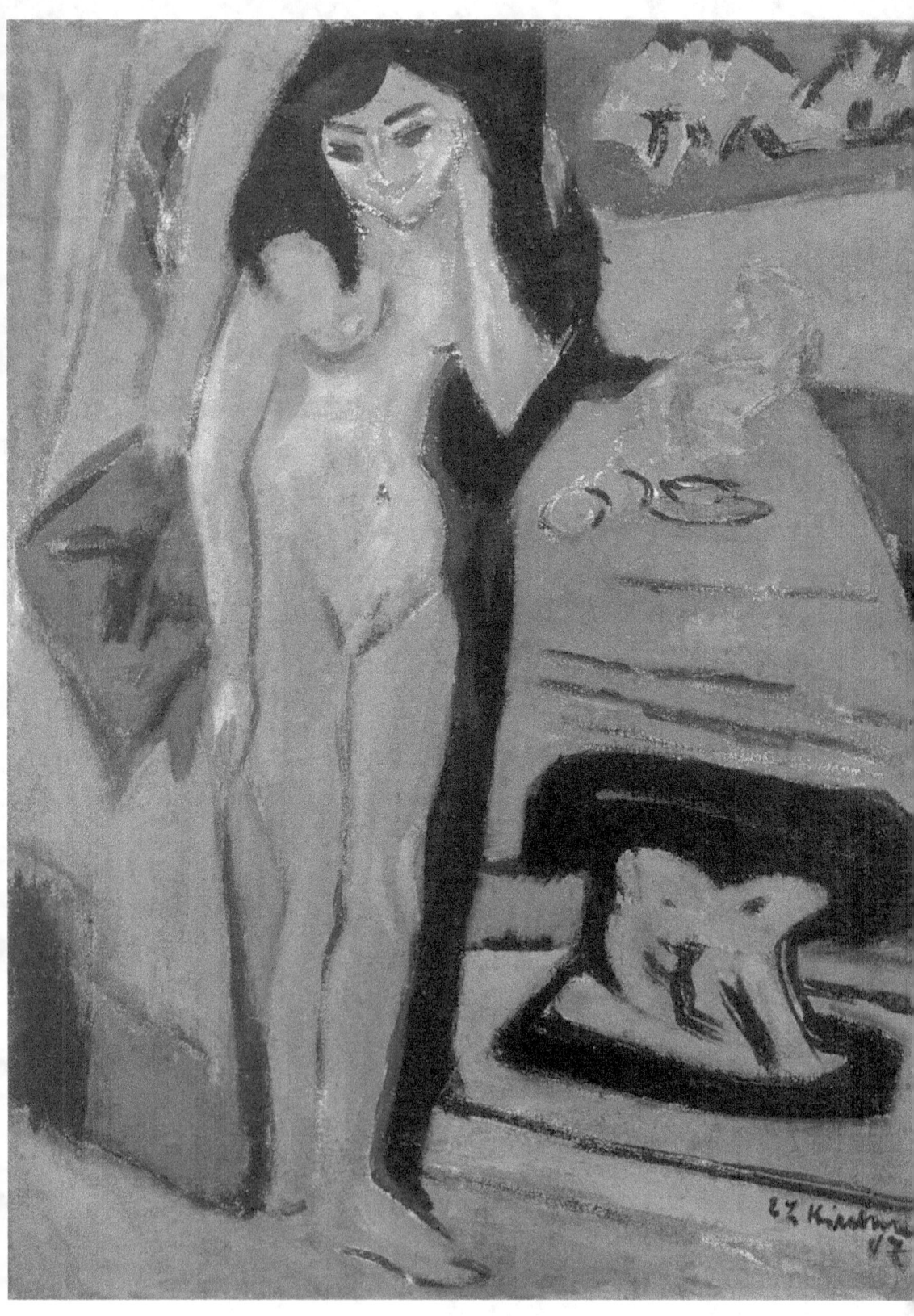

Ernst Ludwig Kirchner, Naked Woman, 1910/ 26, Amsterdam

Notes

2 *Romantic Presence: Brice Marden and the Abstract Expressionists*

1. Suzi Gablik: "Minimalism", in N. Stangos, 245
2. F. Stella, *Working Space*, 123-5
3. F. Stella: *Working Space*, 42

3 *The Art of Brice Marden*

1. P. Gauguin: "Notes Synthetiques", in *Paul Gauguin: A Sketchbook*, tr. Raymond Cogniat, Hammer Galleries, New York, NY, 1962, 57f
2. Maurice Denis: "Definitions of Neotraditionism", 1890, in *Theories: 1890-1910*, Rouart et Watelin, Paris 1920, 5f
3. Quoted in Peter Fuller: "Jasper Johns Interviewed", *Art Monthly*, no 18, July 1978, 12
4. Max Kozloff: "Pop Culture, Metaphysical Designs and the New Vulgarians", *Art International*, March 1962, 34-6
5. Quoted in Michael Crichton: *Jasper Johns*, 21
6. J. Johns, quoted in M. Crichton, 28. See Riva Castleman: *Jasper Johns: A Print Retrospective*, Little, Brown, New York 1986; Richard Field: *Jasper Johns: Prints 1960-1970*, Praeger 1970; Christian Geelhaar: *Jasper Johns: Working Proofs*, Peterborough 1980; D. Shapiro: *Jasper Johns, Drawings*, Abrams, New York, NY, 1984; Judith Goldman: *Jasper Johns: Prints 1977-1981*, Thomas Segal Gallery, Boston
7. Scott Burton: "Reviews and Previews" *Art News*, February 1968

8. F. Stella, radio broadcast, 1964, in Gregory Battock, 158
9. C. Greenberg: "Modernist Painting", 106
10. See M. Fried, *Three American Painters*, 14-15
11. Sheldon Nodelman: "Sixties Art: Some Philosophical Perspectives", *Perspecta: The Yale Architectural Journal*, 11, 1967, 75
12. Jo Baer: "Letters", *Artforum*, vol. 6, no. 1, September 1967, 6
13. C. Greenberg: *Art and Culture*, Beacon Press, Boston 1961, 134
14. L. Fontana, quoted in Jan Van der Marck, *Lucas Fontana*, catalogue, Walker Art Center Minneapolis 1966
15. L. Shearer, 1975, 10
16. C. Ratcliff, 1981, 128
17. Interview, 13 November 1980, in F. Colpitt, 1990, 32

4   *Brice Marden and Minimalism*

1. Jasper Johns: "Sketchbook Notes", in *Art and Literature*, 4, Lausanne, Spring 1965, 192
2. In Leo Steinberg: "Jasper Johns: The First Seven Years of His Art", in *Other Criteria: Confrontations with Twentieth-Century Art*, Oxford University Press, New York, NY, 1972, 31
3. Lawrence Alloway: "Residual Sign Systems in Abstract Expressionism", *Artforum*, November 1973
4. Samuel Wagstaff: "Paintings to Think About", *Art News*, vol. 62, no. 9, January 1964, 62
5. H. Frankenthaler, in E. De Antonio, 77
6. M. Fried: *Three American Painters*, 44
7. See Irving Sandler, *American Art*, 245f, Lucy Lippard: "An Impure Situation", *Art International*, 20 May 1966, 62; Robert Morris: "Notes on Sculpture", op.cit.; Kynaston McShine, 1966; Richard Lund: "Why Isn't Minimal Art Boring?", *Journal of Aesthetics and Art Criticism*, vol. 45, no. 2, Winter 1986, 195-7
8. Lucy Lippard: "New York Letter: Recent Sculpture as Escape", *Art International*, Feb 1966, 50
9. James Mellow: "New York Letter", *Art International*, 20 April 1966, 89
10. Robert Morris: "Notes on Sculpture", part 3, *Artforum* 5, 10, Summer 1967, 29
10. Robert Morris, ib., 29
11. D. Judd, in Kynaston McShine, 1966
12. See Ann Sargent Wooster: "Sol LeWitt's Expanding Grid", *Art in America*, vol. 68, no. 5, May 1980, 143-7
13. Sol LeWitt: "Paragraphs on Conceptual Art", *Art Language*, May 1969. See *Sol LeWitt*, Gemeentemuseum, The Hague 1970; Lucy Lippard: "Sol LeWitt: Non-Visual Structures", *Artforum*, April 1967; Roberta Smith: "Sol LeWitt", *Artforum*, Jan 1975; Ann Sargent Wooster: "LeWitt's Expanding Grid", *Art in America*, May 1980
14. Donald Judd: "Specific Objects", *Arts Yearbook*, 8, 1965, 82

15. Peter Fuller: "The Journey: A Personal Memoir", *Modern Painters*, vol. 3, no. 3, 1990, and in P. Fuller 1993, xxxv

5 *The Abstract Annunciation: Marden's* Annunciation Series

1. Fra Roberto Caracciolo: *Sermones de Laudibus Sanctorum*, Naples 1489, in M. Baxandall, 1988, 51
2. R. Caracciolo, in M. Baxandall, 1988, 51-55
3. Rainer Maria Rilke, *Translations From the Poetry of Rainer Maria Rilke*, tr. M.D. Herter Norton, W.W. Norton, 1993, 208-9
4. B. Marden, in Robin White, 1980
5. 'For the Christian artist the problem of representing divinity has been and still is practically insoluble for no means has yet been found to demonstrate in convincing pictorial form that Christ is God, other than introducing some symbolic element such as the halo. It is for this reason that the masterpieces of Christian art almost never show Christ preaching his messages… but show instead the crucified or resurrected Christ, Christ in majesty, or Christ as judge and ruler of the Universe, since all these epiphanies of Christ could be expressed in comprehensible form. Such restriction of subject matter reflects the difficulty of expressing by artistic means the mystery of the Incarnation, the simple fact that God concealed Himself in human flesh and thereby made Himself no longer recognizable as God.' (Mircea Eliade: "Divinities: Art and the Divine", in 1985, 387).

6 *Multipanel and Monochrome: The Paintings of the 1960s and 1970s*

1. Carter Ratcliffe, 1975, 85; C. Robins, 1984, 183

7 *Greece, the Passion and* Thira

1. L. Durrell, *Reflections on a Marine Venus*, Faber 1960, 183
2. B. Marden, notebook, Hydra, Summer 1974, W, 57
3. B. Marden in R. White, 1980, 13
4. Jeremy Lewison, P, 43; Roberta Smith, W, 52

9 *Brice Marden Goes East*

1. M. Basho, *The Narrow Road to the Deep North and Other Travel Sketches*, tr. Nobuyuki Yuasa, Penguin 1966, 33
2. M. Ueda: *Matsuo Basho*, Twayne, New York, NY, 1970, 167
3. Chuang-tzu, *Basic Writings*, tr. Burton Watson, Columbia University Press, 44

4. Chuang-tzu, *Basic Writings*, 54
5. See Hugh Cumming: "Abstract Painting and the Spiritual" and "The Spiritual in Art: Abstract Painting: Charles Jencks interviews Maurice Tuchman", in A.C. Papadakis, ed. *Abstract Art and the Rediscovery of the Spiritual*, 19f, 42
6. Robert Fludd: *Utriusque cosmi maioris scilicet et minoris metaphysica, physica atque technica historia*, Oppenheim 1617, I, 26
7. John White, 67-69
8. *The Collected Songs of Cold Mountain*, tr. Red Pine, Port Townsend, Washington, 1983

10 Brice Marden and Other Painters

1. See Brenda Richardson: *Frank Stella: The Black Paintings*, Baltimore Museum of Art, Baltimore 1976, 3; F. Colpitt, 29
2. See Carlo Huber: *Robert Ryman*, Kunsthalle, Basle; Nancy Grimes: "Robert Ryman's White Magic", *Art News*, Summer 1968, 86-92; Carter Ratcliff: "Robert Ryman Making Distinctions", *Art in America*, June 1986, 92-97
3. Lynda Nead: "Getting down to basics: art, obscenity and the female nude", in Isobel Armstrong, 206.

Bibliography

BRICE MARDEN

Suicide Notebook, Editions des Masson, Lausanne 1974
Brice Marden: Recent Paintings and Drawings, Pace Gallery, New York, NY, 1978
Brice Marden: Paintings and Drawings, Galerie Valeur, Nagoya, Japan 1980
Paintings, Drawings and Prints 1975-1980, ed. Nicholas Serota, Whitechapel Art Gallery, London, 1981
Brice Marden: Marbles, Paintings, and Drawings, Pace Gallery, New York, NY, 1982
Brice Marden: Recent Work, Pace Gallery, New York, NY, 1984
Reports Notebook, Pace Gallery, New York, NY, 1984
Tu Fu: Thirty-six Poems, tr. Kenneth Rexroth, Peter Blum Edition, New York, NY, 1987
Brice Marden: New Paintings, Mary Boone/ Michael Werner Gallery, New York, NY, 1987
Brice Marden, Galerie Montenay 1987
Brice Marden: recent paintings and drawings, Anthony d'Offay Gallery, London 1988
Brice Marden: The Grove Group, text: Robert Witten, Gagosian Gallery, New York, NY, 1991
Brice Marden: Recent Drawings and Etchings, Matthew Marks Gallery, New York, NY, 1991
Paintings and Drawings, ed. David Whitney, Harry N. Abrams, New York, NY, 1992

Brice Marden: Prints 1961-1991: A Catalogue Raisonné, text: Jeremy Lewison, Tate Gallery, London, 1992

Brice Marden: Paintings, Drawings, Etchings, Matthew Marks Gallery, New York, NY, 1993

Brice Marden, Eva Keller & John Yau. *Brice Marden: Drawings and Paintings 1964-2002*, 2003

Mario Codognato & Brice Marden. *Brice Marden: Works On Paper 1964-2001*, 2004

Lisa Liebmann & Brice Marden. *Brice Marden: Paintings On Marble*, 2005

Jeffrey Weiss & Brice Marden. *Brice Marden: Letters*, 2011

[statements] in J. Lebensztejn

"Three Deliberate Grays for Jasper Johns", *Art Now: New York*, vol. 3, no. 1, March 1971

"Points of View", *Arts Magazine*, vol. 45, no. 3, Dec 1971, 41-42

"Notes: a Mediterranean Painting", in *The Structure of Colour*, Whitney Museum of American Art, New York, NY, 1971, 20

[statement] "Documenta 5: A Critical Preview", ed. Bruce Kurtz, *Arts Magazine,* vol. 46, no. 8, Summer 1972, 43

"Conversation with Brice Marden", ed. Robinson de Ak, *Art Rite*, no. 9, Spring 1975, 39-42

"Five Lines For Klaus", in *Brice Marden*, Kunstraum, Munich, 1979

"Brice Marden Interview", Robin White, in *View*, Crown Point Press, Oakland, California 1980

"The '60s in Abstract Painting: 13 Statements...Brice Marden", *Art in America*, October 1983

OTHERS

William C. Agee: *Don Judd*, Whitney Museum of American Art, New York, NY, 1968

—. *The Sculpture of Donald Judd*, Art Museum of South Texas, Corpus Christi 1977

Edit de Ak *et al*: "Conversations with Brice Marden", *Art-Rite/ Painting*, no. 9, Spring 1975

L. Alloway. "Signs and Surface: Notes on Black and White Paintings in New York", *Quadrum*, 9, New York, NY, 1960,

—. "The American Sublime", *Living Arts*, 1, 2, June, 1963

—. *Morris Louis*, Guggenheim, New York, NY, 1963

—. *Systematic Painting*, New York, NY, 1966

—. "Residual Sign Systems in Abstract Expressionism", *Artforum*, Nov, 1973

A.C. Anderson: "Brice Marden", *Art in America*, June 1973

Carl Andre: "Brice Marden Paintings", *57th Street Review*, 15 Nov 1966

David Anfam: *Abstract Expressionism*, Thames & Hudson, London, 1990
Emile de Antonio & Mitch Tuchman: *Painters Painting*, Abbeville Press, New York, NY, 1984
Richard Armstrong *et al*. *1989 Biennial Exhibition*, Whitney Museum of American Art, New York, NY, 1989
H.H. Arnason: *Robert Motherwell*, Abrams, New York, NY, 1982
John Ashberry: "Gray Eminence", *ARTnews*, vol. 71, no. 1, March 1972, 26-27, 64-66
—. "A Few Choice Openings: Brice Marden", *New York Magazine*, 2 Oct 1978
Geoffrey Ashe: *The Virgin: Mary's Cult and the Re-emergence of the Goddess*, Arkana, London, 1987
—. *Discovering the Goddess: A Personal Testimony*, Crescent Moon 1995
Dore Ashton: *American Art Since 1945*, Thames & Hudson, London, 1982
—. "Introduction", *Brice Marden's Drawings 1963-73*, Contemporary Arts Museum, Houston 1974
—. "Brice Marden: Drawings 1963-1973", *Fort Worth Star-Telegram*, Nov 10, 1974
—. "Young Abstract Painters: Right On!", *Arts Magazine*, Feb 1970
Michael Auping: *Abstraction, Geometry, Painting: Selected Geometric Abstract Painting in America Since 1945*, Abrams, New York, NY, 1989
Patrick Bade: *Femme Fatale: Images of evil and fascinating women*, Ash & Grant, London, 1979
Kenneth Baker: *Minimalism: Art of Circumstance*, Abbeville, New York, NY, 1988
Stephan Bann: *Brice Marden: Paintings, Drawings, Etchings 1975-80*, Stedelijk Museum, Amsterdam 1981
—. "Brice Marden: From the Material to the Immaterial", in Brice Marden: *Paintings, Drawings and Prints 1975-1980*
—. "Adriatics a propos of Brice Marden", *20th Century Studies*, no. 15/16, 116-129
—. "Brice Marden", *Kunstforum International*, April 1987
David Batchelor: "Brice Marden, Anthony d'Offay", *Artscribe*, Dec 1988
Carlo Battaglia: "Tre Artisti: Ryman, Marden, Bell", *QUI Arte Contemporanea*, June 1973
Gregory Battock, ed. *Minimal Art: A Critical Anthology*, Studio Vista, London, 1969
—. "Brice Marden", *Arts Magazine*, Feb 1968
—. "The Moral Integrity of Smudges", *New York Times*, Jan 25, 1968
—. "Art in America: Confusions", *Domus*, March 1975
Michael Baxandall: *Painting and Experience in 15th Century Italy*, Oxford University Press, London, 1988
—. *Patterns of Intention: On the Historical Explanation of Pictures*, Yale University Press 1985
Germain Bazin: *A Concise History of World Sculpture*, David & Charles, Newton Abbot 1981
Nicola Bennett: *The British Art Show: Old Allegiances and New Directions*

1979-1984, Orbis, London, 1984

Maurice Berger: *Labyrinths: Robert Morris, Minimalism and the 1960s*, Harper & Row, New York, NY, 1989

Jane Bell: "Brice Marden", *Art News*, Nov 1978

Tiffany Bell: "Drawing with Respect to Painting", *Arts Magazine*, July 1986

M. Betz: "Brice Marden", *Art News*, Sept 1977, vol. 76, no. 7

Bruce Bolce: "The Quality Problem", *Artforum*, vo. 11, no. 2, October 1972, 68-80

Lizzie Borden: "Cosmologies", *Artforum*, Oct 1972

—. "Brice Marden, Bykert Gallery", *Artforum*, May 1973

Georges Boudaille: *Expressionists*, Alpine Fine Arts Collection, London, 1976

David Bourdon. "The Mini-Conceptual Age", *Village Voice*, 17 Oct 1974

—. "You Can't Tell a Painter By His Colors", *Village Voice*, 24 March 1975

—. "Art: Brice Marden", *Village Voice*, 19 April 1976

—. *Carl Andre: Sculpture 1959-1977*, Jaap Rietman, New York, NY, 1978

Michel Bourel & Sylvie Coudere: *Art Minimal II, De la Surface au Plan*, CAPC Musée d'Art contemporain de Bordeaux 1986

Frederick Brandt: "Brice Marden", in *Late 20th Century Art, Selections from the Sydney and Frances Lewis Collection in the Virginia Museum of Fine Arts*, Virginia Museum of Fine Arts, Richmond 1985

Nina Bremer: "Brice Marden", *Pantheon*, July 1975

Michael Brenson: "Brice Marden's Webs in Action Over a Void", *New York Times*, 15 April 1988

—. "They Seek Spiritual Meaning in Age of Skepticism", *New York Times*, 11 May 1986

Helmut Brinker: *Zen in the Art of Painting*, Routledge & Kegan Paul 1987

Al Brunelle: "Brice Marden", *Art News*, Jan 1969

Judith Bumpus: "Brice Marden: Paintings, Drawings, and Prints 1974-80", *Connoisseur*, May 1981

Edgar Buonagurio: "Brice Marden", *Arts Magazine*, Feb 1979

Titus Burckhardt: *Sacred Art in East and West*, Perennial Book, Middlesex 1967

Nicolas & Elena Calas: *Icons and Image of the Sixties*, Dutton, New York, NY, 1971

John Caldwell: *Carnegie International*, Carnegie Museum of Art, Pittsburgh 1988

Shaun Caley: "Brice Marden", *Flash Art*, Summer 1987

Joseph Campbell: *The Power of Myth*, with Bill Moyers, ed. Betty Sue Flowers, Doubleday, New York, NY, 1988

Barbara Cavaliere: "Brice Marden", *Arts Magazine*, Dec 1978

—. "Brice Marden", *Arts Magazine*, Dec 1980

Germano Celant: "Maleri", *Das Bild einer Geschichte 1956/1976: Die Sammlung Panza di Biumo*, Electa, Milan 1980

—. *Arte come Arte*, Centro Communitario di Brera, Milan 1973

Tom Chetwynd: *A Dictionary of Symbols*, Collins, London, 1982

Herschel B. Chipp, ed. *Theories of Modern Art*, University Press of

California, Los Angeles 1968
J.E. Cirlot: *A Dictionary of Symbols,* Routledge, London, 1981
Frances Colpitt: *Minimal Art: The Critical Perspective,* University of
   Washington Press, Seattle, 1990
J.C. Cooper: *An Illustrated Dictionary of Traditional Symbols,* Thames &
   Hudson, London, 1978
John Coplans: "Post-Painterly Abstraction", *Artforum,* vol. 2, no. 12,
   Summer 1964, 4-9
—. "Serial Imagery", *Artforum,* vol. 7, no. 2, October 1968, 34-43
F. Crichton: "Brice Marden at Hester Royen", *Art International*, April 1975,
   vol. 19, no. 4,
Michael Crichton: *Jasper Johns,* Thames & Hudson, London, 1977
Douglas Crimp: "Opaque Surfaces", in G. Celant 1973
Jean-Luc Daval: *History of Abstract Painting,* Art Data 1989
Guy Davenport: *Artist's Sketchbooks,* Matthew Marks Gallery, New York,
   NY, 1991
Wilfred Dickhoff: "There Is More Than What There Is", in *Brice Marden,*
   Michael Werner, Cologne 1989
W. Domingo: "Brice Marden", *Arts Magazine,* Jan 1971
—. "Color abstraction", *Arts Magazine,* Jan 1971
Joseph Dreiss: "Brice Marden", *Arts Magazine,* June 1974
Wolf-Dieter Dube: *The Expressionists,* Thames & Hudson, London, 1972
Steven C. Dubin: *Arresting Images: Impolitic Art and Uncivil Actions,*
   Routledge, London, 1992
L. Durrell. *Collected Poems 1931-1974,* ed. James A. Brigham, Faber 1980
—. *The Mediterranean Shore: Travels in Lawrence Durrell Country,*
   introduction & commentary by Durrell, Pavilion/ Michael Joseph, 1988
John Elderfield: *Helen Frankenthaler,* New York, NY, 1989
Mircea Eliade: *Ordeal by Labyrinth,* University of Chicago Press 1984
—. *Symbolism, the Sacred and the Arts,* Crossroad, New York, NY, 1985
—. *A History of Religious Ideas*, I, Collins, London, 1979
—. *Patterns in Comparative Religion*, Sheed & Ward, London, 1958
Stephen Ellis: "Brice Marden at Mary Boone", *Art in America,* June 1988
Albert Elsen: *Modern European Sculpture 1918-45,* New York, NY, 1979
John Ferguson: *An Illustrated Encyclopaedia of Mysticism,* Thames &
   Hudson, London, 1976
Jack Flam: "Old Artists, New Styles", *Wall Street Journal,* 25 March 1987
Nina French-Frazier: "Brice Marden", *Art International*, Feb 1981
Peter Fingesten: *The Eclipse of Symbolism*, University Press of California
   1970
Hal Foster: "Brice Marden", *Artforum,* Dec 1980
Richard Francis: *Jasper Johns,* New York, NY, 1984
Elizabeth Frank: "Brice Marden at Pace", *Art in America,* Jan 1981
E. Franz: *Jackson Pollock,* Abbeville, New York, NY, 1983
Michael Fried: *Three American Painters: Kenneth Noland, Jules Olitski,
   Frank Stella,* Fogg Art Museum, Harvard University, Cambridge, Mass.,
   1965

—. *Morris Louis*, Abrams, New York, NY, 1970

—. "Art and Objecthood", *Artforum*, 5, Summer 1967, 12-23

Peter Fuller: *Peter Fuller's Modern Painters: Reflections on British Art*, ed. John McDonald, Methuen, London, 1993

Gary Garrels, Brenda Richardson, Richard Shiff & Brice Marden. *Plane Image: A Brice Marden Retrospective*, 2006

Matilda Ghyka: *The Geometry of Art and Life*, Sheed & Ward, New York, NY, 1946

Eric Gibson: "Brice Marden", *Art International*, Nov 1978

Pamela Church Gibson & Roma Gibson, ed. *Dirty Looks: Women, Pornography, Power*, British Film Institute, London, 1993

Jeremy Gilbert-Rolfe: "Brice Marden's Paintings", *Artforum*, vol. 13, no. 2, Oct 1974, 30-38

—. "Brice Marden", *Artforum*, June 1974

—. "Brice Marden, David Novros, Bykert Gallery", *Artforum*, May 1974

Pat Gilmour: "Brice Marden", *Arts Review*, 22 May 1981

Bruce Glaser: "Questions to Stella and Judd", ed. Lucy Lippard, *Art News*, vol. 65, no. 5, September 1966, 55-61

Grace Glueck: "Brice Marden", *New York Times*, 3 Dec 1966

—. "From Master to Modular", *Art in America*, Dec 1970

Tony Godfrey: *The New Image: Painting in the 1980s*, Phaidon, London, 1986

—. "The Human Presence in Recent Abstract Painting", *Aspects*, Fall 1979

—. "Brice Marden at the Whitechapel", *Artscribe*, June 1981

Amy Golin: "Brice Marden", *Art News*, Dec 1966

—. "Brice Marden", *57th Street Review*, 15 Nov 1966

Jane Gollin: "Brice Marden", *Art News*, Nov 1966

Robert Goldwater & Marco Treves, eds. *Artists on Art*, John Murray, London, 1975

Clement Greenberg: "Modernist Painting", *Arts Yearbook*, 4, Art Digest, New York, NY, 1961, 100-8

—. *Post-Painterly Abstraction*, Los Angeles County Museum, Los Angeles 1964

John Gruen: "Brice Marden", *New York Magazine*, 30 Nov 1970

Marlis Gruterich: "Brice Marden", *Heute Kunst*, Oct 1973

Kathy Halbreich: *Affinities: Myron Stout, Bill Jensen, Brice Marden, Terry Winters*, Hayden Gallery, MIT, Cambridge 1983

Niki Hale: "Of a Classic Order: Brice Marden's Thira", *Arts Magazine*, vol. 55, no. 2 October 1980, 152-3

—. "Marden's Greek Landscape", *Art/World*, Oct-Nov 1980

James Hall: *A Dictionary of Subjects and Symbols in Art*, John Murray 1984

Susan Harris: "Brice Marden", *Arts Magazine*, Jan 1985

Judith Helfer: "Abstralte Kunst – Reduziert, Brice Marden", *Aufbau*, 28 March 1975

Adrian Henri: *Environments and Happenings*, Thames & Hudson, London, 1974

Fabrice Hergott: "Brice Marden", *La Collection du Musée,* Editions du

Centre, Paris 1986
Gerrit Henry: "Brice Marden", *Art News*, Jan 1983
Hayden Herrera: "Brice Marden", *Art News*, Summer 1974
—. "Brice Marden, David Novros (Bykert, Downtown)", *Art News*, April 1974
Thomas Hess: *Barnett Newman*, Walker, New York, NY, 1969
—. "Rules of the Game: Part II: Marden and Rockburne", *New York Magazine*, 11 Nov 1974
—. "Brice Marden", *New York Magazine*, 7 April 1975
Robert Hewison: *Future Tense: A New Art For the Nineties*, Methuen, London, 1990
Ann Hindry: "Brice Marden", *Artstudio*, Summer 1986
Janet Hobhouse: *The Bride Stripped Bare: The Artist and the Nude in the Twentieth Century*, Cape, London, 1988
Ingeborg Hoesterey: "Brice Marden", *Art International*, 15 June 1975
Roman Hollenstein: "Brice Marden", in Jean-Christophe Ammann, *Von Twombly bis Clemente: Selected Works from a Private Collection*, Kunsthalle, Basle 1985
Klaus Honnef: *Contemporary Art*, Benedikt Taschen, Cologne 1988
Sam Hunter, ed. *An American Renaissance: Painting and Sculpture Since 1940*, Abbeville Press, New York, NY, 1986
—. *American Art of the 20th Century*, Thames & Hudson, London, 1973
Waldemar Januszczak, ed. *Techniques of the World's Great Painters*, Phaidon, London, 1980
D. Judd. "Frank Stella", *Arts Magazine,* 36, Sept, 1962
—. "Black, White and Gray", *Arts Magazine*, 38, 6, Mch, 1964
—. "Specific Objects", *Arts Yearbook*, 8, Art Digest, New York, NY, 1965
—. *Complete Writings, 1959-1975*, Nova Scotia College of Art and Design, Halifax, Canada, 1975
—. *Complete Writings, 1975-1986*, Van Abbemuseum, Netherlands, 1987
C.G. Jung: *Memories, Dreams, Reflections*, Collins, London, 1967
S. Kappeler: *The Pornography of Representation*, Polity Press, Cambridge 1986
Hermann Kern: "Brice Marden: Painter and Graphic Artist", in *Brice Marden Drawings 1964-78*, Kunstraum, Munich 1979, 12-18
Klaus Kertess: "The Drawings of Brice Marden", in *Brice Marden Drawings 1964-78*, Kunstraum, Munich, 1979, 12-18
—. "Drawing Conclusions", *Brice Marden*, Galerie Montenay, Paris 1987
—. "Painting Hot Staying Cool", *Elle*, Nov 1991
—. "Plane Image: The Painting and Drawing of Brice Marden", in PD
M. Kimmelman: "Matthew Marks, New York: recent drawings and etchings", *New York Times*, 24 May 1991, C26
—. "Brice Marden Reveals His Connections", *New York Times*, 14 April 1991
Max Kozloff: *Jasper Johns*, New York, NY, 1969
—. "New York Letter", *Art International*, vol. 8, no. 3, April 1964
Hilton Kramer: "Marden at the Guggenheim", *New York Times*, 15 March

1975
—. "Brice Marden", *New York Times*, 10 Oct 1980
Rosalind E. Krauss: *Passages in Modern Sculpture*, Thames & Hudson, London, 1977
Julia Kristeva: *The Kristeva Reader*, ed. Toril Moi, Blackwell, London, 1986
—. *Desire in Language: A Semiotic Approach to Literature and Art*, ed. Leon Roudiez, tr. Thomas Gora, Alice Jardine & Leon Roudiez, Blackwell, London, 1982
Janet Kutner: "Brice Marden, David Novros, Mark Rothko: The Urge to Communicate through Non-Imagistic Painting", *Arts Magazine*, vol. 50, no. 1, Sept 1975, 61-63
Weston La Barre: *The Ghost Dance*, Allen & Unwin, London, 1972
Philip Larson: "Brice Marden", in *Painting: New Options*, Walker Art Center, Minneapolis 1972
—. "Minneapolis: Brice Marden at Locksley/Shea", *Arts Magazine*, Jan 1979
—. "Avant to Be in Style", *Village Voice*, 8-14 Oct 1980
Jean-Claude Lebensztejn: *Brice Marden*, Pace Gallery, New York, NY, 1978, 3-7
—. "Mumû: Autour de Cinq 'Annunciations' de Marden", *Avant-Guerre*, no. 1, 1980
—. "Sans Titre (Oceanique)" in *Brice Marden*, Galerie Montenay 1987
Dennis Leder: "5 Annunciations", *America*, 3 Feb 1979
Lisa Liebmann: "Brice Marden: the Duse of Minimalism", *Parkett*, no. 7, January 1986
Richard Lind: "Why Isn't Minimal Art Boring?", *Journal of Aesthetics and Art Criticism*, vol. 45, no. 1, Winter 1986
Kate Linker: "Abstraction: Form as Meaning", in Singerman 1986
Lucy Lippard: *From the Center: feminist essays on women's art*, Dutton, New York, NY, 1976
—. *Ad Reinhardt*, Abrams, New York, NY, 1981
—. *Six Years: The Dematerialization of the Art Object from 1966 to 1972*, Praeger, New York, NY, 1973
—. "The Silent Art", *Art in America*, vol. 55, no. 1, Jan-Feb 1967, 58-63
—. "Rebelliously Romantic?", *New York Times*,4 June 1967
Ulrich Loock: "Brice Marden – Plane Image", *Arts*, Nov 1989
Edward Lucie-Smith: "Brice Marden", *Art International*, Sept 1981
S.H. Madoff: "The Return of Abstraction", *Arts News*, Jan 1986
Dorothy Mayall: *The Minimal Tradition*, Aldrich Museum of Contemporary Art, Ridgefield, Conn., 1979
Sarah McFadden: "Brice Marden", in J. Caldwell
Donald McKinney: *Yves Klein, Brice Marden, Sigmar Polke*, Hirschl & Alder Modern, New York, NY, 1989
Kynaston McShine: *Primary Structures*, Jewish Museum, New York, NY, 1966
J.C.J. Metford: *Dictionary of Christian Lore and Legend*, Thames & Hudson, London, 1983
Dorothy C. Miller, ed. *Sixteen Americans*, MOMA, New York, NY, 1959

Toril Moi: *Sexual/ Textual Politics: Feminist Literary Theory*, Routledge, London, 1988

Anna Moszynska: *Abstract Art*, Thames & Hudson, London, 1990

Laura Mulvey: *Visual and Other Pleasures*, Macmillan, London, 1989

Robert Murdoch: *Modular Painting*, Albright-Knox Art Gallery, Buffalo 1970

Lynda Nead: *Female Nude: Art, Obscenity and Sexuality*, Routledge, London, 1992

Terry A. Neff, ed. *A Quiet Revolution: British Sculpture Since 1965*, Thames & Hudson, London, 1987

Barnett Newman: *Stations of the Cross*, Guggenheim, New York, NY, 1966

Sheldon Nodelman: *Marden, Novros, Rothko: Painting in the Age of Actuality*, Institute for the Arts, Rice University, Houston 1978

Gerald Nordland: *Fourteen Abstract Painters*, Frederick S. Wright Art Gallery, University of California, Los Angeles 1979

Rudolf Otto: *The Idea of the Holy*, Oxford University Press, London, 1958

Erwin Panofsky: *Studies in Iconology*, Harper & Row, New York, NY, 1972

Andreas C. Papadakis, ed. *The New Romantics*, Art & Design (vol 4 11/12), Academy Group, London, 1988

—. ed. *British and American Art: The Uneasy Dialectic*, Art & Design (vol 3 9/10), Academy Group, London, 1987

—. ed. *Abstract Art and the Rediscovery of the Spiritual*, Art & Design (vol 3 5/6), Academy Group, London, 1987

Michael Payne: *Reading Theory: An Introduction to Lacan, Derrida, and Kristeva*, Blackwell, London, 1993

Francesco Pellizzi: "For Brice Marden: twelve fragments on surface", *Parkett*, no. 7, January 1986

Jeff Perrone: "Review", *Artforum*, December 1976

Michael Phillipson: *Painting, Language and Modernity*, Routledge 1978

Robert Pincus-Witten: "Systematic Painting", *Artforum*, vol. 5, no. 3, November 1966, 42-45

—. "Ryman, Marden, Manzoni: Theory, Sensibility, Mediation", *Artforum*, vol. 10, no. 10, June 1972, 50-53

Maurice Poirier: "Color-coded Mysteries", *ARTnews*, January 1985

—. & Jane Necol: "The '60s in Abstract Painting: 13 Statements...Brice Marden", *Art in America*, October 1983

Earl A. Powell: "Brice Marden", in *The James A. Michener Collection: 20th Century American Painting*, University of Texas, Austin 1977

Mel Ramsden: "Jeremy Gilbert-Rolfe's as-silly-as-you-can-get 'Brice Marden's Painting'", *The Fox*, no. 2, April 1975, 8-14

Carter Ratcliff: *In the Realm of the Monochrome*, Renaissance Society, University of Chicago, Chicago 1979

—. "Mostly Monochrome", *Art in America*, vol. 69, no. 4, April 1981, 111-131

—. "Once More With Feeling", *ARTnews*, vol. 71, no. 4, Summer 1972, 35-7, 67-9

—. "Abstract Painting, Specific Spaces: Novros and Marden in Houston", *Art in America*, vol. 63, no. 5, November, 1975

Brian Redhead: *The Inspiration of Landscape: Artists in National Parks*, Phaidon 1989

Kathleen J. Reiger, ed. *The Spiritual Image in Modern Art*, Theosophical Publishing House, Wheaton, Illinois 1987

Ad Reinhardt: *Art as Art: The Selected Writings of Ad Reinhardt*, University of California Press, Berkeley, 1991

K. Rexroth. *One Hundred Poems From The Chinese*, New Directions Books, New York, NY, 1971

Brenda Richardson. *Brice Marden: Cold Mountain*, Menil Collection, 2007)

Dippel Rini: "Fundamental Painting", in *Fundamental Painting*, Stedelijk Museum, Amsterdam 1975

Corinne Robins, ed. *The Pluralist Era: American Art 1968-1981*, Harper & Row, New York, NY, 1984

—. "Empty Paintings", *SoHo Weekly News*, 22 April 1976

Barbara Rose: "ABC Art", *Art in America*, vol. 53, no. 5, November 1965, 57-69

—. *American Art Since 1900*, Thames & Hudson, London, 1967

—. *American Painting*, Skira/ Rizzoli International, New York, NY, 1986

Harold Rosenberg, *The Tradition of the New*, Da Capo Press, New York, NY, 1994

Robert Rosenblum: *Frank Stella*, Penguin, London, 1971

—. *Modern Painting and the Northern Romantic Tradition*, Thames & Hudson, London, 1978

—. *Jasper Johns' Paintings and Sculptures 1954-1974*, Ann Arbor, Michigan 1985

Stephanie Rosenthal. *Black Paintings: Robert Rauschenberg, Ad Reinhardt, Mark Rothko, Frank Stella*, 2007

Mark Rothko: *Mark Rothko 1903-1970: A Retrospective*, Guggenheim, New York, NY, 1979

David S. Rubin: "History", *Contemporary Triptychs*, Montgomery Art Gallery, Pomona College, Claremont, California 1982

Lawrence Rubin: *Frank Stella Paintings: 1958-1965*, New York, NY, 1986

William S. Rubin: *Frank Stella*, New York Graphic Society, Greenwich, Conn., 1970

—. *Frank Stella: 1970-1987*, MOMA, New York, NY, 1987

Bertrand Russell: *A History of Western Philosophy*, Allen & Unwin 1971

Irwin Sandler: *The Triumph of American Painting*, Harper & Row 1970

—. *American Art of the 1960s,* Harper & Row, New York, NY, 1988

Jean-Paul Sartre: *Being and Nothingness, tr.* Hazel Barnes, Methuen, London, 1969

Christoph Schenker: "Brice Marden", in *Dokumentation 5*, InK, Halle fur Internationale Neue Kunst, Zurich, 1980

Peter Schjeldahl: *Art in Our Time: The Saatchi Collection*, Lund Humphries, 1984

—. "Contemporary American Art", in T. Vuorikoski

—. "Marrying Abstraction", in Brice Marden, 1987

Eric Shanes: *Constantin Brancusi*, Abbeville, New York, NY, 1989

David Shapiro & Cecil Shapiro, eds. *Abstraction Expressionism: A Critical Record*, Cambridge University Press, London, 1990

Linda Shearer: *Brice Marden*, Guggenheim, New York, NY, 1975, 9-27

Patterson Sims: "Brice Marden" in *Whitney Museum of American Art: Selected Works*, Whitney Museum of American Art, New York, NY, 1985

Howard Singerman, ed. *Individuals: A Selected History of Contemporary Art, 1945-1986*, Museum of Contemporary Art, Los Angeles 1986

Brydon Smith: *Donald Judd*, National Gallery of Canada, Ottawa 1975

David Smith: *Sculpture and Drawings*, ed. Jörn Merkert, Prestel-Verlag, Munich 1981

Roberta Smith: "Brice Marden's Paintings", *Arts Magazine*, vol. 47, no. 7, June 1973, 30-41

—. "Brice Marden", in Brice Marden: *Paintings, Drawings and Prints 1975-1980*

Elke M. Solomon: *Recent Drawings: William Allan, James Bishop, Vija Celmins, Brice Marden, Jim Nutt, Alan Saret, Pat Steir, Richard Tuttle*, American Foundation of Art, New York, NY, 1975

Naomi Spector: *Robert Ryman*, Whitechapel Art Gallery, London, 1977

Nikos Stangos, ed. *Concepts of Modern Art*, Thames & Hudson, London, 1981

Frank Stella: *Working Space*, Harvard University Press, Cambridge, Mass., 1986

Susan Rubin Suleiman, ed. *The Female Body in Western Culture: Contemporary Perspectives*, Harvard University Press, Cambridge, Mass., 1986

Nina C. Sundell: "Brice Marden", in *The Robert and Jane Meyerhoff Collection: 1958-1979*, Jane B. Meyerhoff, Baltimore 1980

S. Tallman: "The other biennial", *Arts Magazine*, vol. 64, no. 6, Feb 1990

Joshua Taylor *et al*: *Robert Rauschenberg*, Smithsonian Institute, Washington 1976

Tu Fu: *Thirty-Six Poems*, tr. Kenneth Rexroth, with 25 etchings by Brice Marden", Peter Blum, New York, NY, 1987

Maurice Tuchman: *The New York School*, Thames & Hudson, London, 1971

—. *The Spiritual in Art: Abstract Painting 1880-1985*, Los Angeles County Museum of Art/ Abbeville Press, New York, NY, 1986

Jan van der Marck: *American Art: Third Quarter Century*, Seattle Art Museum, Washington 1973

Paul Vogt: *Contemporary Painting*, Abrahams, New York, NY, 1981

Timo Vuorikoski, ed. *Amerikkalaista Nyktaidetta/ Amerikkansk Samtidskunst/ Contemporary American Art*, Sarah Hilden Art Museum, Tampere, Finland 1988

Diane Waldman: *Mark Rothko*, Thames & Hudson, London, 1978

Daniel Wheeler: *Art Since Mid-Century: 1945 to the Present*, Thames & Hudson 1991

John White: *The Birth and Rebirth of Pictorial Space*, Faber, London, 1957/87

Robin White: "Interview with Brice Marden", in *View*, Crown Point Press, Oakland, California 1980

Mara R. Witzling: *Voicing Our Visions: Writing by Women Artists*, Women's Press, London, 1992

Heinrich Wolfflin: *Classic Art*, Phaidon, London, 1952/80

Gerard Woods *et al*, eds. *Art Without Boundaries*, Thames & Hudson 1972

John Yau: "Introduction to the Etchings", in B. Marden 1987

—. "A Vision of the Unsayable", in B. Marden 1988

William Zimmer: "Marden 1982: Hermeticism Made Visible", in *Brice Marden,* Pace Gallery, New York, NY, 1982

ARTS, PAINTING, SCULPTURE

The Art of Andy Goldsworthy: Complete Works
Andy Goldsworthy: Touching Nature
Andy Goldsworthy in Close-Up
Andy Goldsworthy: Pocket Guide
Andy Goldsworthy In America
Land Art: A Complete Guide
The Art of Richard Long: Complete Works
Richard Long: Pocket Guide
Land Art In the UK
Land Art in Close-Up
Land Art In the U.S.A.
Land Art: Pocket Guide
Installation Art in Close-Up
Minimal Art and Artists In the 1960s and After
Colourfield Painting
Land Art DVD, TV documentary
Andy Goldsworthy DVD, TV documentary
The Erotic Object: Sexuality in Sculpture From Prehistory to the Present Day
Sex in Art: Pornography and Pleasure in Painting and Sculpture
Postwar Art
Sacred Gardens: The Garden in Myth, Religion and Art
Glorification: Religious Abstraction in Renaissance and 20th Century Art
Early Netherlandish Painting
Leonardo da Vinci
Piero della Francesca
Giovanni Bellini
Fra Angelico: Art and Religion in the Renaissance
Mark Rothko: The Art of Transcendence
Frank Stella: American Abstract Artist
Jasper Johns
Brice Marden
Alison Wilding: The Embrace of Sculpture
Vincent van Gogh: Visionary Landscapes
Eric Gill: Nuptials of God
Constantin Brancusi: Sculpting the Essence of Things
Max Beckmann
Caravaggio
Gustave Moreau
Egon Schiele: Sex and Death In Purple Stockings
Delizioso Fotografico Fervore: Works In Process 1
Sacro Cuore: Works In Process 2
The Light Eternal: J.M.W. Turner
The Madonna Glorified: Karen Arthurs

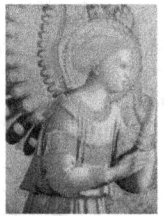
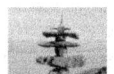
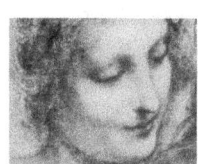
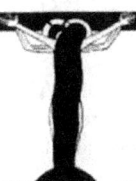
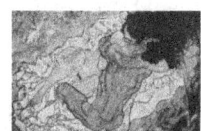

LITERATURE

J.R.R. Tolkien: The Books, The Films, The Whole Cultural Phenomenon
J.R.R. Tolkien: Pocket Guide
Tolkien's Heroic Quest
The *Earthsea* Books of Ursula Le Guin
Beauties, Beasts and Enchantment: Classic French Fairy Tales
German Popular Tales by the Brothers Grimm
Philip Ullman and *His Dark Materials*
Sexing Hardy: Thomas Hardy and Feminism
Thomas Hardy's *Tess of the d'Urbervilles*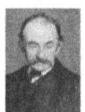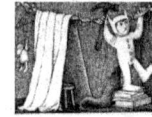
Thomas Hardy's *Jude the Obscure*
Thomas Hardy: The Tragic Novels
Love and Tragedy: Thomas Hardy
The Poetry of Landscape in Hardy
Wessex Revisited: Thomas Hardy and John Cowper Powys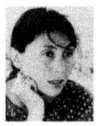
Wolfgang Iser: Essays and Interviews
Petrarch, Dante and the Troubadours
Maurice Sendak and the Art of Children's Book Illustration
Andrea Dworkin
Cixous, Irigaray, Kristeva: The *Jouissance* of French Feminism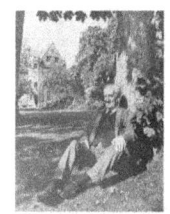
Julia Kristeva: Art, Love, Melancholy, Philosophy, Semiotics and Psychoanalysis
Hélène Cixous I Love You: The *Jouissance* of Writing
Luce Irigaray: Lips, Kissing, and the Politics of Sexual Difference
Peter Redgrove: Here Comes the Flood
Peter Redgrove: Sex-Magic-Poetry-Cornwall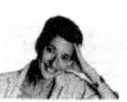
Lawrence Durrell: Between Love and Death, East and West
Love, Culture & Poetry: Lawrence Durrell
Cavafy: Anatomy of a Soul
German Romantic Poetry: Goethe, Novalis, Heine, Hölderlin
Feminism and Shakespeare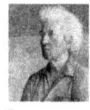
Shakespeare: Love, Poetry & Magic
The Passion of D.H. Lawrence
D.H. Lawrence: Symbolic Landscapes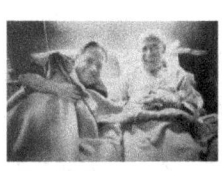
D.H. Lawrence: Infinite Sensual Violence
Rimbaud: Arthur Rimbaud and the Magic of Poetry
The Ecstasies of John Cowper Powys
Sensualism and Mythology: The Wessex Novels of John Cowper Powys
Amorous Life: John Cowper Powys and the Manifestation of Affectivity (H.W. Fawkner)
Postmodern Powys: New Essays on John Cowper Powys (Joe Boulter)
Rethinking Powys: Critical Essays on John Cowper Powys
Paul Bowles & Bernardo Bertolucci
Rainer Maria Rilke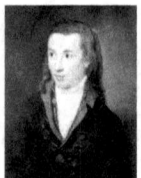
Joseph Conrad: *Heart of Darkness*
In the Dim Void: Samuel Beckett
Samuel Beckett Goes into the Silence
André Gide: Fiction and Fervour
Jackie Collins and the Blockbuster Novel
Blinded By Her Light: The Love-Poetry of Robert Graves
The Passion of Colours: Travels In Mediterranean Lands
Poetic Forms

POETRY

Ursula Le Guin: Walking In Cornwall
Peter Redgrove: Here Comes The Flood
Peter Redgrove: Sex-Magic-Poetry-Cornwall
Dante: Selections From the Vita Nuova
Petrarch, Dante and the Troubadours
William Shakespeare: Sonnets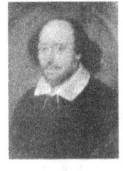
William Shakespeare: Complete Poems
Blinded By Her Light: The Love-Poetry of Robert Graves
Emily Dickinson: Selected Poems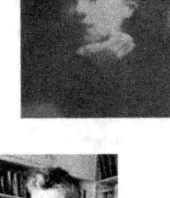
Emily Brontë: Poems
Thomas Hardy: Selected Poems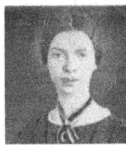
Percy Bysshe Shelley: Poems
John Keats: Selected Poems
Joh n Keats: Poems of 1820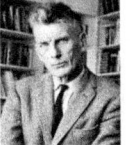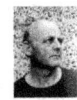
D.H. Lawrence: Selected Poems
Edmund Spenser: Poems
Edmund Spenser: Amoretti
John Donne: Poems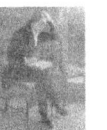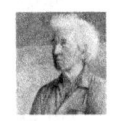
Henry Vaughan: Poems
Sir Thomas Wyatt: Poems
Robert Herrick: Selected Poems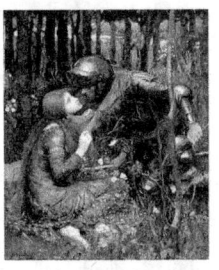
Rilke: Space, Essence and Angels in the Poetry of Rainer Maria Rilke
Rainer Maria Rilke: Selected Poems
Friedrich Hölderlin: Selected Poems
Arseny Tarkovsky: Selected Poems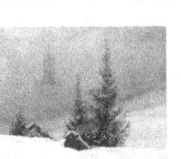
Arthur Rimbaud: Selected Poems
Arthur Rimbaud: A Season in Hell
Arthur Rimbaud and the Magic of Poetry
Novalis: Hymns To the Night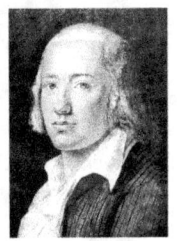
German Romantic Poetry
Paul Verlaine: Selected Poems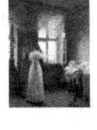
Elizaethan Sonnet Cycles
D.J. Enright: By-Blows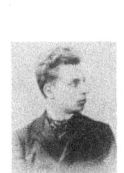
Jeremy Reed: Brigitte's Blue Heart
Jeremy Reed: Claudia Schiffer's Red Shoes
Gorgeous Little Orpheus
Radiance: New Poems
Crescent Moon Book of Nature Poetry
Crescent Moon Book of Love Poetry
Crescent Moon Book of Mystical Poetry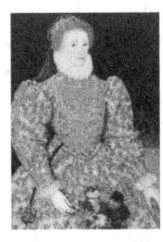
Crescent Moon Book of Elizabethan Love Poetry
Crescent Moon Book of Metaphysical Poetry
Crescent Moon Book of Romantic Poetry
Pagan America: New American Poetry

MEDIA, CINEMA, FEMINISM and CULTURAL STUDIES

J.R.R. Tolkien: The Books, The Films, The Whole Cultural Phenomenon
J.R.R. Tolkien: Pocket Guide
The *Lord of the Rings* Movies: Pocket Guide
The Cinema of Hayao Miyazaki
Hayao Miyazaki: *Princess Mononoke*: Pocket Movie Guide
Hayao Miyazaki: *Spirited Away*: Pocket Movie Guide
Tim Burton
Ken Russell
Ken Russell: *Tommy*: Pocket Movie Guide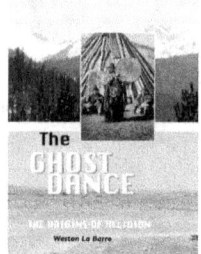
The Ghost Dance: The Origins of Religion
The Peyote Cult
Cixous, Irigaray, Kristeva: The *Jouissance* of French Feminism
Julia Kristeva: Art, Love, Melancholy, Philosophy, Semiotics and Psychoanalysis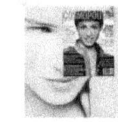
Luce Irigaray: Lips, Kissing, and the Politics of Sexual Difference
Hélene Cixous I Love You: The *Jouissance* of Writing
Andrea Dworkin
'Cosmo Woman': The World of Women's Magazines
Women in Pop Music
Discovering the Goddess (Geoffrey Ashe)
The Poetry of Cinema
The Sacred Cinema of Andrei Tarkovsky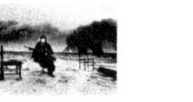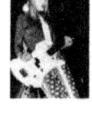
Andrei Tarkovsky: Pocket Guide
Andrei Tarkovsky: *Mirror*: Pocket Movie Guide
Andrei Tarkovsky: *The Sacrifice*: Pocket Movie Guide
Walerian Borowczyk: Cinema of Erotic Dreams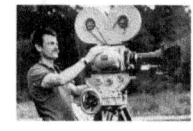
Jean-Luc Godard: The Passion of Cinema
Jean-Luc Godard: *Hail Mary*: Pocket Movie Guide
Jean-Luc Godard: *Contempt*: Pocket Movie Guide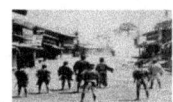
Jean-Luc Godard: *Pierrot le Fou*: Pocket Movie Guide
John Hughes and Eighties Cinema
Ferris Bueller's Day Off: Pocket Movie Guide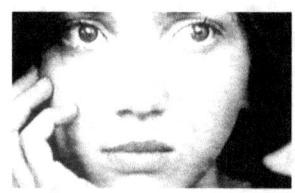
Jean-Luc Godard: Pocket Guide
The Cinema of Richard Linklater
Liv Tyler: Star In Ascendance
Blade Runner and the Films of Philip K. Dick
Paul Bowles and Bernardo Bertolucci
Media Hell: Radio, TV and the Press
An Open Letter to the BBC
Detonation Britain: Nuclear War in the UK
Feminism and Shakespeare
Wild Zones: Pornography, Art and Feminism
Sex in Art: Pornography and Pleasure in Painting and Sculpture
Sexing Hardy: Thomas Hardy and Feminism

In my view *The Light Eternal* is among the very best of all the material I read on Turner. (Douglas Graham, director of the Turner Museum, Denver, Colorado)

The Light Eternal is a model monograph, an exemplary job. The subject matter of the book is beautifully organised and dead on beam. (Lawrence Durrell)

It is amazing for me to see my work treated with such passion and respect. (Andrea Dworkin)

CRESCENT MOON PUBLISHING
P.O. Box 1312, Maidstone, Kent, ME14 5XU, Great Britain. www.crmoon.com

www.ingramcontent.com/pod-product-compliance
Lightning Source LLC
Chambersburg PA
CBHW051310220526
45468CB00004B/1281

* 9 7 8 1 8 6 1 7 1 3 7 6 6 *